# The Discovery of Tahiti

## Joan Druett

## *The Discovery of Tahiti*

AN OLD SALT PRESS BOOK, published by Old Salt Press, a Limited Liability Company registered in New Jersey, U.S.A.
For more information about our titles, go to
*www.oldsaltpress.com*

© 2018 Joan Druett

ISBN 13: 978-0992258856

Cover photograph of Moorea from the sea © Ron Druett 2017

# The Discovery of Tahiti

## Joan Druett

*"Swaying palms, warm blue waters lapping gently on pristine white beaches, dramatic mountains draped in dense forest, tropical flowers and welcoming locals"*

– travel brochure

*"Honeymooning or not, the South Pacific is a marvelous place for romantic escapes. After all, romance and the islands have gone hand-in-hand since the bare-breasted young women of Tahiti gave rousing welcomes to the 18th-century European explorers"*

– Frommers

*"...almost suddenly, so overwhelmingly, was the idea of the Pacific at last to enter into the consciousness, not of seamen alone but of literate Europe ... For Wallis had not merely found a convenient port of call. He had stumbled on a foundation stone of the Romantic movement"*

– J. C. Beaglehole

The day Tahiti was recognized as romantic paradise was the same day the lookout of the British frigate *Dolphin* spied Deal Castle rising from the mists of Dover, and shouted, "Land ho for home!"

It was dawn, and the low sun cast wrinkled shadows on the patched, grimy sails as they were taken in, one by one. When the ship was close to shore, orders were gruffly called out, and the seamen, seasoned by many long months at sea, moved with the economy of habit. The anchor was dropped with a splash in a swirl of widening ripples, and the *Dolphin* bounced as she was caught up by the chain, then gradually stilled. Briskly, a boat was lowered, and the captain was sculled to the waterfront. Not long after the boat returned without him, he could be glimpsed on a hired horse, hurrying out for London with a satchel full of reports, and the crew settled down to wait.

Just a few more moments later, a voice called out from the water below the starboard side of the ship. It was a reporter from *Lloyds List*, who had the job of rowing out a little boat to each newly anchored vessel, to make routine queries about the ship's name, the captain's name and the name of the last port visited. Today, this man was especially curious, because the *Dolphin* was an interesting vessel, having been on a mysterious mission.

He was not allowed on board, because the ship had to be passed by the "Clerk of the Cheque" before visitors were permitted, but the seamen readily abandoned their work about the decks to gather at the rail and call out replies to his flow of increasingly informal questions. They had strict orders from Captain Wallis to keep quiet about where they had been, but the captain was not there, the journalist was an attentive listener, and the first lieutenant was too sick to stop their tongues rattling. So tales of an idyllically beautiful south sea island were spun, along with lingering descriptions of doe-eyed, half-naked Tahitian maidens with mischievously writhing hips.

These lovely native girls were astoundingly generous with their favors, the journalist learned, and winsomely grateful for the gift of an iron nail in return. These "Otaheite" people had a queen, the seamen confided further, a statuesque and commanding woman. Her name was Oberea, and she had fallen in love with their skipper, Captain Samuel Wallis — a tubby little man with neither the bearing nor the reputation of a hero. Indeed, or so they said, she adored him so greatly that when he informed her that he was determined to sail away, she collapsed to the ground, prostrated with grief, and "the last Thing she did was to take the Crown from her own Head" and present it to him.

Unsurprisingly, the reporter rowed away in a hurry, and in London the headlines were read with riveted interest, while the trumpets of the newspaper vendors wailed even more loudly than usual in the streets. It was only natural, too, after the pilot finally came on board and the ship took the flood tide for the Thames, that her progress should be tracked by men from other papers.

2

Seamen who would have normally gazed about from their stations on the deck and in the rigging, beset with the strange feeling of disassociation that comes over men who are coming home after a long time at sea, had no time to feel alien or lonely, because they had so much attention from the press.

All around them ships were beating into port, while others were flowing out under full sail, on the way to Spithead, but for once these were paid scant regard. The river was also crowded with bustling colliers, barges, hoys, and two-masted tilt boats, but, more importantly for the *Dolphin* crew, rowboats sculled by reporters were threading through the throng. As evening fell, the bastions of Tilbury Fort bobbed into view, and then the timber-framed waterfront taverns of Gravesend. The *Dolphin* dropped anchor for the night, and the off-duty crew crowded into the taverns, where rapt listeners paid for their tales with ale.

The day that the ship arrived with her enlivening news was May 19, 1768. Otherwise unremarkable in history, it is a date that marks a sea-change in the way Europeans pictured the Pacific.

It was the day that the world found out about Tahiti.

# Chapter 1:
# Terra Australis Incognita

According to European history, the Pacific Ocean was discovered by a man on a mountain.

The date was September 25, 1513, and the man, Vasca Núñez de Balboa, had battled marsh and jungle to cross the Isthmus of Panama and clamber to the top of that hill. The story goes on to relate that he was so dazzled by what he saw that he fell to his knees and thanked God for the privilege of being the man to discover this great ocean.

Naturally, he had no idea that the ocean had already been discovered by others — that it was strewn with islands that teemed with a nation of the greatest natural navigators the world has ever known, people who had made their own great voyages, which were memorialized in legend and song. As far as Balboa knew, and the Western world was concerned, the great south sea was just an empty space on the map of the world, which had to be explored to be filled.

Meantime, it was filled with dreams. Lurking some-where in that ocean was a great continent that would yield new goods and new markets, and add even more luster to the empire that could claim its discovery — or so the intelligentsia of Europe were convinced. According to the theory that was first formulated by the Greek philosopher, Aristotle, it had to be there, to balance the weight of Europe, Russia, and Asia in the north. Furthermore, it was supposed to be mild in climate, rich in gold and iron ore, extremely fertile, and inhabited by some mysterious race of interesting people. This imaginary continent even had a name, *Terra Australis Incognita*, and was placed on many European charts, just as if it was really there.

No sooner was the great south sea recognized, than sailors started searching for this fabled realm. In 1519, six years after Balboa dropped to his knees on a Panama hilltop, a Portuguese soldier by the name of Ferdinand Magellan set out with five ill-equipped galleons, to find a way to sail into the ocean by steering about the bottom of South America. Battling winds, calms, terrified crews and his own hostile Spanish captains (Magellan arranged the murder of one, executed another, and marooned a third), he discovered and negotiated the straits that were named in his honor. After finally emerging into the Pacific he crossed it, but his only landfalls before arriving at Guam were two tiny uninhabited atolls. Magellan's great discovery was that the Pacific was *vast*: over the fifteen weeks that it took to cross the ocean, his men were reduced to gnawing leather chafing gear, and nineteen died of scurvy and starvation.

Following his course was better than taking the risk of getting lost in the uncharted ocean, though, so for some years his desolate path from the Pacific end of Magellan's Strait was the only seaway from South America to the East Indies. Another maritime highway was established in 1565, when Spanish pilots found a route that the Manila Galleons — the ships carrying silver and gold from Mexico to the East, and returning with legendary cargoes of silks, spices, precious stones, and porcelain — could sail, but this was in another empty stretch of sea where there were no islands to find.

The great extent of the Pacific remained as unfamiliar as ever, but visions of fabulous riches kept men venturing into unknown waters. In 1567, impelled by Inca stories of Tupac Yupanqui — who, according to legend, had sailed to the west and returned with gold, silver, and slaves — a Mendaña-led expedition set out from New Spain (Mexico) in a quest for Solomon's land of Ophir in the western Pacific. They did find some islands, which have been called the Solomon Islands ever since, but because it was so difficult to fix longitude at the time, they lost the islands again.

Then English privateers joined the hunt.

The outbreak of the War of the Austrian Succession, in 1739, gave the English corsairs an excuse to hunt Spanish shipping in the Pacific, the treasure-laden Manila Galleon being a particular goal. A naval operation was organized, and George Anson - brother-in-law of the Lord Chancellor, and a man who had served twice as a captain on the North American station - was appointed as commodore. He was given six ships - *Centurion, Gloucester, Severn, Pearl, Wager* and *Tryal*, plus two hired storeships, *Anna* and *Industry* - but because of the demands of the war they were seriously undermanned. When Anson complained, 260 invalids were sent from the Chelsea Hospital, most over sixty years old, and many so weak that they had to be hoisted on board. After another protest, 210 completely untrained, newly recruited marines arrived.

Badly supplied in all respects, the squadron sailed from England in September 1740. Gales battered the ships from the first moment they entered the Atlantic, and the passage to Madeira, which normally took about ten days, took forty. Soon after leaving the island, the captain of the storeship *Industry* asked to be relieved of his charter, then trans-shipped all the stores to the other ships, loading them so deep in the water that the scuttles that provided

7

fresh air to the berth decks could not be propped open. Vermin thrived in the dank, airless, insanitary conditions, and lice-borne typhus swept through the fleet.

Worse was to come. Within days of reaching Cape Horn, so many men were dead of scurvy that officers had to do the work of common seamen. The men died "like rotten sheep," as a lieutenant phrased it, the official account describing "ulcers of the worst kind, attended with rotten bones, and such a luxuriancy of fungous flesh, as yielded to no remedy."

The symptoms appeared about six weeks after the fresh provisions ran out. The first was an unnatural lassitude, which was followed by a rash of purple spots on the legs, that ran together until the swollen limbs turned black. Old wounds that had healed broke open, and bones that had knitted fractured again. The gums became spongy, and teeth dropped out, while at the same time blood trickled out of the nostrils and eye-sockets. Without fresh fruit and vegetables, death was inevitable, as bleeding inside the skull caused the brain to compress and literally explode.

By the time George Anson weighed anchor at the first Pacific rendezvous, the island of Juan Fernández, his fleet had been reduced to just four ships. The *Severn* and the *Pearl* had given up and turned back, and the *Wager* had been wrecked. And, of the original crews of the survivors, which had totaled 961, six hundred and twenty-six were dead.

Anson carried on, seizing several Spanish prizes and burning the port of Paita, losing more ships and more men as he progressed. By May 1742, only the *Centurion* and the *Gloucester* were still afloat, and in August so few seamen were fit to work that Anson was forced to take the *Gloucester*'s survivors on board the flagship, and scuttle the decaying hulk.

Days later, his one-ship expedition dropped anchor at Tinian, an island in the Spanish Marianas, where a further twenty-one died in the last stages of scurvy.

In October 1742, Anson sailed for Macao to get the *Centurion* ready for ambushing the Manila Galleon in the Philippine Islands. On June 20, 1743, the Manila Galleon *Nuestra Señora de la Covadonga* was raised, and was immediately engaged. There were not enough gunners to service the cannons for a broadside, so the gangs ran from one gun to another, firing at will as they went.

Not only did this erratic bombardment confuse the Spanish, but the *Centurion*'s men, all hardened survivors of one of the worst voyages on record, fought with grim ferocity - with such brutal effect that by the time the Spanish captain gave up and yielded his ship, along with its fabulous cargo, he had lost more than sixty killed and seventy wounded.

And George Anson had lost just two — for a haul of 1,313,843 pieces of eight, and 35,682 ounces of pure silver. So, despite his appalling losses to typhus and scurvy, he arrived home to a hero's welcome.

This dramatic story of awful failure metamorphosing into resounding success led to a clarion call for further discovery, sounded in 1744 by the influential writer and thinker, Dr John Campbell. England was in the middle of a commercial explosion, he argued, and the bounds of her trade should be extended into new, as yet undiscovered lands.

She had the manufactories, the shipping, the seamen, the bankers, and the brokers, so all that was necessary was new outlets for her goods, he declared. "*If we search, we will find; if we knock, it will be opened,*" was his catch cry.

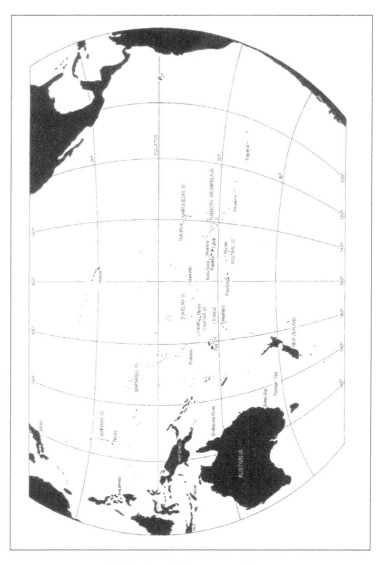

*Pacific Ocean* © *Ron Druett 2012*

Campbell's campaign took on impetus the following year, 1745, when the first account of Anson's trans-Pacific voyage was published. While the venture had wreaked a horrifying cost in terms of both ships and men, he argued, in commercial terms the expedition had been a resounding triumph. Alone, and seriously undermanned, the *Centurion* had captured the kind of prize that had not been seen since the time of Francis Drake, the queen's corsair. And it was a triumph that should be emulated, repeated again and again!

Understandably, in view of this, the Admiralty paid due attention when Anson recommended that the passage about Cape Horn should be secured by establishing a base in the south Atlantic where British ships could shelter and refresh. The choice was either a mythical island known as "*Pepys's*," which had been "laid down by Dr. *Halley*," or the almost equally unknown Falklands.

As Anson said, possession of one or both of these would make the British "masters of those seas," his idea being strategic as well as commercial. The Admiralty immediately began to make plans for an expedition, but unfortunately the Spanish heard of it. Having read Anson's account, *A Voyage round the world*, they detected the imperialist motives behind the move, and protested.

So, as the British government was anxious to re-establish good relations with Spain, the project was shelved, leaving the geographers to their speculations about the land that lay somewhere in the great south sea, with the French academicians, Paris being the centre of cartography, very much at the hub of the debate.

And then, in 1760, young George III ascended the British throne.

The young man who was crowned in 1760 bore little resemblance to the apparently demented monarch who eventually lost the American colonies. Just twenty years old, well educated, intelligent, and altruistic, the new king had a keen interest in the exploration of the unknown parts of the globe. His was the enthusiasm that led to new expeditions "to make Discoveries of countries hitherto unknown."

No sooner had the Treaty of Paris ended the Seven Years' War than the Admiralty was instructed to make plans for another expedition. It was decided that it should be made up of two ships, a frigate and a consort.

And so the frigate *Dolphin* entered history.

*Dolphin and deck plans © Ron Druett 2012*

# DOLPHIN

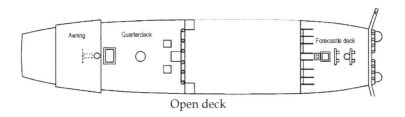

Open deck

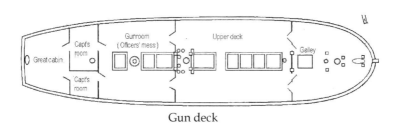

Gun deck

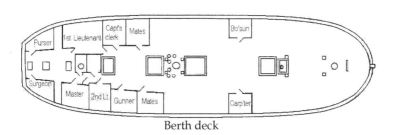

Berth deck

Hold and stores

13

Built in Woolwich Dockyard in 1751, HMS *Dolphin*, rated at 508 tons, was a sixth rate frigate, pierced for 24 cannon on her gundeck, with eight more guns out in the open on her quarterdeck. There were no guns on her berth deck, which meant that the seamen did not have the usual inconvenience of slinging their hammocks around great iron cannon. Considering her small size (113 feet long, and 32 feet wide) and her large complement of 160, the frigate *Dolphin* was surprisingly comfortable.

Topsides, she had an unusually long quarterdeck, 55 feet long, which was partly roofed over with a big wooden awning, making it a pleasant promenade for the captain and the officer on watch, being a shelter from both the rain and the sun. At the stern, two quartermasters (seamen who steered the ship) stood at the wheel, guided by the compass, which was set in a steadying binnacle. The capstan, which was used to weigh the anchors, and was worked by seamen pushing on bars as they trudged round the central barrel, stood on the forward, unsheltered part of the quarterdeck, between the mizzen (sternmost) mast and the main (middle) mast. There were four guns on either side of this.

The next deck down was the gun deck. Right at the stern of this deck was the Great Cabin, which was the captain's domain. Here, he could work on his charts and draughts, and take his meals, either alone or with invited company from shore, or from the officers' ranks, at sea. Two small cabins ran forward from this, one being Captain Wallis's stateroom, where he slept, and the other his dressing room, which had a toilet with an outlet to the sea.

A marine stood sentry between the two doors that led from these cabins to the next room forward, which was the gunroom. On most navy ships of the time the gunroom was the place where the midshipmen lived, but journals make it clear that on the *Dolphin* it was where the officers and petty officers had their meals. It was an airy place, as it had gunports for the cannon that ranged along each side, and which were turned sideways and lashed out of the way when the guns were not in action.

Two doors at the front of the gunroom led to gangways that were built along the sides of the deck, leaving an open space in the middle where the ship's boats were stored, inside one another, on spars. Right forward on this deck was the ship's kitchen, or galley, which was under the shelter of the forecastle deck, and was furnished with a giant iron stove.

The next deck down was the berth deck, where most of the ship's complement lived. Little cabins, each about six feet square, were built at the privileged sternward end, and here the lieutenants, sailing master, purser, gunner, surgeon, and captain's clerk slept, and the "mates" who helped the sailing master, the surgeon, and the gunner mates bunked in shared accommodation. Forward of them, the marines swung their hammocks, while the seamen lived in groups of six - "messes" - in the bows. Here, there were also two extra cabins for the boatswain ("bo'sun") and the carpenter.

The hold, packed with stores for a long voyage, was right at the bottom of the hull. Separate rooms held tools and gear for the carpenter, bo'sun, gunner and sailmaker, with another for the captain's personal goods. The "slop chest" — the store of clothes and items like soap and tobacco that were sold to the men — was also held here, and was the responsibility of the purser, who kept the accounts, assisted by the steward.

Down there, in the bowels of the ship and well below the waterline, the purser worked in a dank space that was lit only by smoky lamps. Here, as in the berth deck, headroom was scant, with a great risk of cracking one's head on heavy beams — reputedly the reason for so many cases of insanity in the navy.

There is no record of anyone complaining about the accommodations, however. In the East End of London living conditions were a lot worse, and here, on board the *Dolphin*, the men were guaranteed three meals a day.

Because of the official interest in the expedition, a lot of care was taken when the *Dolphin* and her consort, the sloop *Tamar*, were readied. The planks at the bottom of the hull of the *Dolphin* were found to be rotten, and replaced with new ones. Then the entire bottom was sheathed with sheets of copper — a revolutionary move that meant the ship was immune from the depredations of shipworm, a kind of barnacle that ate away at wood in temperate waters.

The job that the Admiralty and King George had in mind for the ship was the discovery of a northwest passage across the top of America, which (if found) was an alternative route between the Atlantic and the Pacific, but there were always expressed hopes that they would blunder over the Great Unknown Continent, too. However, fatefully, the man who was appointed as commodore of the two-ship fleet was cautious in the extreme. Where the dashing nature of a determined discoverer was needed, that spirit was distinctly lacking.

This was the Honourable John Byron (the brother of the notorious lord), who had been a seventeen-year-old midshipman on George Anson's expedition, and still had nightmares about it. He had not just watched men suffer and die from scurvy on the passage through the Atlantic and about Cape Horn, but had also been one of the castaways after the *Wager* had run onto icy rocks on the south-western coast of Chile. His account of the ordeal tells a horrifying story of pillaging, drunkenness, treachery and desertion — the crew, reckoning that their contract with the Admiralty ended when the ship was lost, embarked on a free-for-all that ended in fighting and murder. The captain, Lieutenant David Cheap, progressively lost his mind, and eventually descended into a starving travesty of a man, his memory gone, his beard as long as a hermit's, covered with thousands of ants.

They all went hungry. The "sellery" plants and "scurvy grass" (a kind of borage) they foraged on shore cured their scurvy, but did not provide enough calories to keep them alive. When starvation threatened, the castaways split into two desperate groups. Eighty men took a lengthened boat and headed up the Straits of Magellan to the Atlantic. When they eventually arrived at the Rio Grande, their number had been reduced to thirty.

Twenty men, including Byron and Captain Cheap, were left behind. Of these, only four survived, to be delivered by Indians to the Spanish garrison on the bleak island of Chiloe, off the western tip of South America. And there, for the next three years, they were kept prisoner until they were finally sent on French ships to England, where John Byron arrived almost five years after the wreck of his ship.

Little wonder, then, that when he was given command of this new expedition, he persuaded the First Lord of the Admiralty, John Perceval, the second Earl of Egmont, to authorize him "to purchase Vegetables at all such places" he might touch, and "to cause the Ships Companys to be served any quantity of Provisions, beyond the established allowance" whenever he thought necessary.

To make space for these, the beer ration was replaced with brandy, as brandy took up less room, a development that must have greatly pleased the 250 men who crewed the two ships of the expedition. Not only might they make history, but the brandy would warm their bellies.

On June 21, 1764, the *Dolphin* sailed from Portsmouth, trailed by her consort, *Tamar*, which was commanded by Captain Mouat. First, they steered for Madeira (where Byron bought huge quantities of onions and pumpkins), and then voyaged from there to Rio de Janeiro.

Ignoring his instructions, which were to enter the Pacific via the Cape of Good Hope, Byron then steered down the coast of Patagonia to the entrance to the Magellan Straits. There, he dropped anchor at Port Famine, an uninhabited bay that had been given this name because back in the 1580s three hundred Spanish settlers had starved to death there.

Despite this grim history, Byron found it bountiful, rhapsodizing that the men gathered "Fish enough every day for both Ships Companies," with as many geese and ducks as they could shoot. He then sailed to the Falklands, which he claimed for Britain, unaware that the French general, Louis de Bougainville, had done the same for France the year before.

After that, Byron sailed through the Straits of Magellan to the Pacific. Once he arrived in the ocean, he was supposed to head up the coast of North America in his quest for the fabled Northwest Passage, but, being an independent-minded fellow, he headed west. As he blithely confessed in his logbook, he was bound on a personal search for the fabled Solomon Islands, which Alvaro Mendaña had discovered in 1568, and then lost.

Instead of finding the islands of legendary riches, Byron blundered over a few atolls in the Tuamotus, which he formally called "Queen Charlotte Islands," but referred to as "the Islands of Disappointment." He had several good reasons for this — the ships could find no anchorage, the inhabitants strongly resisted landings, and there was little to forage for the boats that did get on shore, save a few coconuts and the local scurvy grass. He was not even able to boast that he was the discoverer, as one of the officers found the "carved Head of a Dutch Long boats Rudder" — a remnant from the *African Galley*, one of the ships of an expedition headed by Roggeveen, which had wrecked there in 1721.

A few days later, on June 28, 1765, "Finding there is no such Land as laid down ... for Solomon's Islands," Byron gave up and steered north for Tinian, the same island in the Marianas where Anson had rested his scurvy-ridden seamen. After resting his own sick men (who all recovered), Byron then sailed through the South China Sea to Batavia (modern Jakarta), and from there to the Cape of Good Hope. After another spell to refresh his crews, he took his departure for home, where he arrived in May 1766, having discovered nothing at all.

This was much to the disgust of commentators in England, one of whom wrote, "the necessary inference is that Byron was wanting in the instinct and hound-like perseverance that go to make up the great discoverer."

But John Byron was a survivor, and also a pioneer in something that was far more important, which he passed on to his successor, Samuel Wallis — the determined foraging for anti-scorbutic herbs, even on the most daunting shores.

Samuel Wallis © Ron Druett, 2018

Scurvy grass

# Chapter 2 :
# "The well known Streight we Enter then"

While the Honourable John Byron's voyage had been yet another demonstration that the Pacific was, in fact, a broad and empty ocean, an entry in his journal persuaded the geographers and the Admiralty that *Terra Australis Incognita* really did lurk somewhere in the great south sea.

Dated June 16, 1765, it read:

> *For a day or two before we made the Islands of Disappointment till this day ... we saw vast flocks of Birds which we observed towards Evening always flew away to the S°ward. This is convincing proof to me that there is Land that way, & had not the Winds failed me ... I make no doubt but I should have fell in with, & in all probability made the discovery of the S° Continent.*

If Byron's position (latitude 14°17' south, longitude 158°15' west) was correct, then the birds were flying to some island (Tongareva, perhaps) in the Cook Islands, but his assumption that they were returning to their roosts on the coast of *Terra Australis Incognita* persuaded the Admiralty to send out the *Dolphin* on another attempt to find the continent.

21

George III was particularly keen, master's mate Robert Molyneux noting on the front leaf of the journal he kept on this second *Dolphin* expedition that "His Majesty was graciously pleased to authorize this second expedition to be undertaken, in hopes of finding a continent of great extent never yet explored or seen between the Streights of Magellan and New Zealand."

Understandably, in view of his failure to follow orders, John Byron was not appointed to the command again — and had great trouble getting the authorities to pay the men's extra allowances and approve his lavish spending on fresh provisions, too. Instead, the Admiralty selected a Cornishman, 38-year-old Samuel Wallis.

Wallis was such an insignificant fellow that it is hard to guess why the choice was made. Born in 1728 in Lanteglos-by-Camelford, a hamlet in Cornwall, he was the son of minor gentry, and his only patron was Admiral Boscawen, whom he had served as flag lieutenant during the 1744-1749 war with France. For the three years since the Peace of Paris, he had been floating about on half-pay, so it must have been quite a surprise for him to be summoned back to duty, as the commander of HMS *Dolphin*.

Never, at any stage in his career, had he expressed any interest in exploration. He also must have felt doubts about the ship he was assigned for this strange job, as the *Dolphin* was only just back from Byron's circumnavigation of the world. When he took her over, however, he was assured that the ship was in excellent shape. Being so interesting, she had been inspected minutely, the shipwrights being particularly concerned about how her copper sheathing had fared.

While the copper was still in good condition, the iron bolts that secured it were very corroded, which could have been a worry. While the foreman did not understand that it was the effect of electrolytic action, he was shrewd enough to recommend that they should be replaced by bolts made of forged copper. Then the rest of her was checked and refurbished, at a total cost of £3,602.16. 4d.

Most of her crew was replaced, though one hardened adventurer by the name of John Gore signed up again. It seems that he was so keen that he was willing to take a demotion. While he had been a sailing master's mate on the Byron voyage, and taken a hand in navigating the ship, he was mustered as an able seaman under Wallis. But one of the peculiarities of the Georgian navy was a certain vagueness in how the junior officers and mates were ranked in the muster book. While Gore had been a petty officer under Byron, he had controlled a watch as second lieutenant, and though the muster book on the second voyage merely ranked him as a seaman, he was one of Wallis's three most important deck officers.

The other deck officers were William Clarke, the first lieutenant, and Tobias Furneaux, the second lieutenant. The master (or sailing master), who was in charge of the set of the sails, and the navigation of the ship, particularly when entering difficult and unknown anchorages, was George Robertson, a large, confident, flamboyant man who was addicted to writing. Throughout the Wallis voyage he produced vivid, racy, wonderfully misspelled descriptions of events on board and his various experiences in Tahiti, plus logbook entries, commentaries and navigational tables.

The master's mate who helped him in his duties was Robert Molyneux, while the list of "young gentlemen" included Richard Pickersgill, who was considered particularly promising. The unusually caring and talented surgeon, John Hutchinson, had a strong interest in antiscurvy measures and the distillation of fresh water. And, remarkably, the purser, John Harrison, was a gifted mathematician with an up-to-date knowledge of celestial navigation.

Samuel Wallis, then, had every reason to be satisfied with both his ship and his crew. Unfortunately, he did not have the same luck with his consort.

The *Tamar* was not available for this second expedition, as her rudder had been so severely damaged during the passage from the Cape of Good Hope that Byron had sent her to Antigua for repairs. Instead, the sloop *Swallow* had been requisitioned, and Philip Carteret, who had been one of Byron's lieutenants, was the man put in command.

Carteret was a very good choice; the ship was not. Built back in 1745, the *Swallow* had been lying neglected in the Medway ever since. When she was surveyed in 1763, she was found to be gravely in need of repairs, which were not done until it was decided that she should be Wallis's consort, and then were carried out in a great hurry. Carteret described her in tones of disgust as "one of the worst if not the very worst of her kind; in his majesty's Navy."

As soon as the two ships left Plymouth, on August 21, 1766, it became plain that her progress through the Atlantic was going to be very slow indeed. Wallis's log from Madeira to the Magellan Straits is a litany of frustration, because he had to reduce canvas constantly, to let the *Swallow* keep up. It was not until December 17, 1766, after a nail-biting creep down the Atlantic, that the two ships finally arrived at the entrance of the Straits.

There were two reasons to be glad — not just that the Straits had at last lay ahead, despite the sluggishness of the poor *Swallow*, but there was an enduring and exciting legend attached to the local Patagonian Indians, meaning that everyone was eager to see them.

Over two centuries earlier, in June 1520, Magellan had called the country "Patagonia" — meaning "Big Foot" — because of the "gigantic" Indians he had encountered there. And it does seem logical that to a five-foot, under-nourished Spanish seaman, a husky Indian measuring something over six feet would indeed seem tall. However, the dimensions were greatly exaggerated after those who had survived Magellan's voyage got home. Pigafetta, the chronicler of the expedition, declared that he came only waist-high to these giants, an outrageous statement that flew around Europe, inspiring huge public interest. Patagonian "Brobdingnagians" entered the literature, and the Pacific was more scary than ever. Not only was the ocean terrifyingly unknown, but its gateway was guarded by ogres.

The myth was reinforced by none less than Captain John Byron, who reported in a letter to Lord Egmont, written at Port Famine, that he had seen Indians "who in size come the nearest to Giants of any People I believe in the world." One of his midshipmen, Charles Clerke, reported to the Royal Society that "there was hardly a man there less than eight feet, most of them considerably more." This was most definitely tongue-in-cheek, because he admitted at the same time that his story was told with "embellishment of truth," but a lot of people believed it, including members of parliament.

Accordingly, the crew of Wallis's *Dolphin* all rushed to the deck when some Indians came galloping along the beach at sunset. Wrote Robertson, "They all appeard very tall Stout Men, which makes us suppose they are the same people which Commander Byron saw." Furthermore, their voices were very loud, "more like Bulls Bellowing or Lyons Roaring nor the Common Size of Men hollowing or talking. This made us all Earnestly wish for a New Day," he added, "that we might have the pleasure of seeing with our own Eyes what sort of People this Patagonians is."

While George Robertson was very willing to believe in outsized men; Samuel Wallis was not. Being too pragmatic to see Clerke's joke, he marched on shore with a measuring stick, and, as he wrote, "and measured more than twenty" of the tallest. Of these "very stout People, few of them if any under six feet; many six feet six inches and one six feet seven inches," or so he found.

So that, he said, was that.

His men, being human, entertained their audiences with tall yarns when they got home, but Wallis flatly refused to cater to the public craving for sensationalism. The ship's barber, Rogers Richardson, wrote a "poetical essay" on the homeward leg of the voyage, and presented it to Wallis, who copied it into his logbook.

"To West our course we steer," — Richardson wrote:

> *"The well known Straights, we enter than,*
> *So fam'd for it's Gigantick Men,*
> *Whose height from six Feet reach'd to ten,*
> *And safely anchor there.*

And Wallis, in the margin of the poem, noted firmly that "ten" meant "six feet ten inches," not ten feet.

SOUTH AMERICA

Buenos Aires · Montevideo

Magellan Strait

Falkland Islands

Tierra del Fuego

Strait of la Maire

Staten Island

Cape Horn

*Falkland Islands and Magellan Strait*
*Map © Ron Druett 2014*

On January 17, 1767, their provisions topped up with fresh game and curative herbs, and having accomplished this measurement of the Patagonian "giants," Captains Wallis and Carteret set out to negotiate the Straits of Magellan to the Pacific. It was a slow slog, because the *Swallow* made such poor progress against the prevailing westerly gales that stormed down the narrow, winding passage. Twice, she nearly wrecked, and altogether she performed so poorly that Carteret volunteered to leave the expedition, and return to England. It was a gallant offer, but one that Wallis turned down.

While both ships battled the tides, the gales, the snow and the hail, a grueling routine was established. The cutter, under the charge of the *Dolphin*'s master, George Robertson, was sent ahead of the two ships, with the job of sounding depths and charting the rocks and reefs, to make sure the next stage of the passage was safe. Then, at night, they would return, cold, frozen, and hungry, but with the report that gave a safe route a few miles further into the straits.

The cuttersmen were not the only ones to spend hours exposed to the cold, sleet, and wind, for men in other boats were foraging the beaches for herbs, meanwhile. These were abundant, happily for the health of the crews, Wallis writing on February 4, "here is likewais great plenty of Sellery, Nettles & scurvy grass of which we daily give to the Ships Company."

But there were other problems. The weather was so wet and dank that by March the sails were mildewed and rotting. Because the passage was taking so much longer than anticipated, their store of food was running low, and foraging for mussels became a priority.

"This Day put the Ships Company to two thirds allowance of all Species of provisions Except Spirits," Wallis noted on March 10; "gave the Capt$^n$ of the Swallow orders to do the same."

At last, on April 11, 1767, the *Dolphin* broke out into the Pacific, to be struck at once by yet another gale. "I would have shortened sail for the *Swallow*," he wrote, "but it was not in my power." A current was dragging them onto the shore, and he had to beat against this and a westerly wind, and so he had to power on, leaving his consort behind.

> *Soon after we lost sight of the Swallow and never saw her afterward. At first I was inclined to have gone back into the straight, but a fog coming on, and the sea rising very fast, we were all of opinion that it was indispensably necessary to get an offing as soon as possible*
>
> — Wallis, logbook on the *Dolphin*, April 11, 1767
>
> *I forgot to mention that we got down four of our foremast Guns and four of the aftermost at Port Famin, in order to keep the ship from Straining her upper works, indeed I may say from Straining her whole frame of the Ship .... At this time we hade a very great Swell from the S.W. which obliged us to carie sail in order to keep the Ship eased and prevent her rowling too mutch in the hollow of the Seas. This made us get so farr ahead of the poor Dull Swall., who was not able to go Above two foot to our three when we hade a mind to carie Sail. What becam of the Swallow after this I know not, as we neather saw nor heard any more of her*
>
> — Robertson, journal, *Dolphin*, April 11, 1767

The *Dolphin* forged on alone. The appalling weather continued — "not a dry Hammock in the Ship," wrote Wallis on 24 April. They were in unknown waters, with no charts, and with limited provisions. On May 13, a man named John Smith committed the unbelievable crime of throwing his messmates' dinner overboard. Wallis ordered a run of the gauntlet, and watched as Smith's angry messmates beat him, then sent them his own dinner to make up for what they had lost.

"Serve Mustard & Vinegar to the People every week & Boil Portable Soup every day with the Pease & Oatmeal," Wallis wrote the same day. All of these were considered of some use against the dreaded scurvy. Mustard was stocked because it was the same color as oranges, which had been recognized since Elizabethan times as a cure for the disease, but unfortunately could not be preserved long at sea, and vinegar valued because it was acid, like lemons. Portable soup was dried meat broth, which made a tasty soup when mixed with hot water, but had none of the vitamins necessary to prevent or cure scurvy.

Now that the "sellery" that had been harvested in the Magellan Strait and had served them so well was no longer obtainable, the threat of the disease loomed large. On June 3: "People begin to fall down of the Scurvy fast, they look sallow and unhealthy," wrote Wallis. Casks of sauerkraut were hoisted up from the hold and broken open, and the pickled cabbage accompanied every serving of meat, "to each mess a proper portion." But, much to his despair, this was as useless as the mustard, soup, and vinegar.

All the old seafarers knew and feared scurvy. During Drake's circumnavigation of the Atlantic in 1585, he lost a quarter of his men to the deficiency disease. In 1657 the

Manila galleon *San Jose* was found drifting off Acapulco, a ghost ship inhabited by dead men. Richard Hawkins, the Elizabethan sea-rover, called scurvy "the plague of the sea, and the spoil of mariners" — and Wallis would have heartily agreed.

Like all good shipmasters, he knew that the only remedy was fresh fruit and vegetables, but there was no hope of getting any until he found a fertile island. To make the situation even worse, both he and his first officer, William Clarke, fell ill with some kind of bilious complaint, caused by the rotting food and foul water that was all they had on board. So, meantime, a strict watch was kept out for land, and the guns and small arms were exercised in case the inhabitants were hostile, while Wallis checked and rechecked his navigational calculations.

And then, to the great relief of all, a string of atolls was raised.

The blobs of land were so low on the water that the *Dolphin* found them by accident. The date (according to sea-time, which was half a day earlier than land-time) was June 7, 1767, the seventh Sunday after Easter, so the first island was named "Whitsun" in the holiday's honor.

Foraging parties were sent ashore, headed by Furneaux, the only fit officer on board. The boats returned with coconuts and scurvy grass, but nothing else of use. Lieutenant Furneaux reported seeing two canoes, but they had swiftly paddled away. So, while there were local inhabitants, they were going to be hard to approach. And until there was some kind of friendly contact, it would be impossible to trade.

Over the next twelve days one atoll after another was visited, and every time the parties that rowed ashore had the same suspicious reception. At some landings the

31

inhabitants fled in a panic, while at others  groups of natives confronted the boats at the beach; these, though they grudgingly traded a few coconuts, would not allow the Europeans to come on shore.

Wallis, thinking he at least had the benefit of discovery, named these unpromising islets after personages back in England — Queen Charlotte, Duke of Gloucester — but in reality he was not the first, or even the third, European voyager to touch this island group, the Tuamotus. As far back as 1615, a Dutch ship, *Eendracht*, with the brothers Schouten and Jacob le Maire on board, had sent a boat on shore at an atoll that they called "Honden" — "Dog" — because the only inhabitants were three dogs; in 1722 another Dutch expedition, headed by Jacob Roggeveen, had lost one of their three ships, the *African Galley*, on a Tuamotu island. The local people scavenged the wreck for iron nails, because they found they were useful for turning into fishhooks and tools, and made excellent trade when bartered at other islands, and so iron became valued throughout eastern Polynesia.

This was the same island where Byron's had party found an old rudder head, but were unable to trade for fresh fruit and vegetables. "This news was great grief to us," as Byron wrote, for his "People" were falling down fast with scurvy, "& several of my best Men already so bad in it, that they are confined to their Hammocks."

Wallis, in these more southern islets of the archipelago, had better luck, as his boats' parties were able to forage for some coconuts, scurvy grass and purslane, though the high surf made it difficult to land. There was also a hint that the native women found the European seamen intriguing. At the atoll they touched on June 18, there were women, "Handsome & dress'd in white," in the crowd gathered on the beach.

When the officer in charge threw the girls "some Beads & Trinketts," it triggered an eager rush, but, as Wallis wrote, "the Men prevented them, & sent them up the Cliff." Attempts to trade followed, but though the seamen in the boats waited several hours, no coconuts or pigs arrived, and so they returned to the ship.

Once they were back on board, Wallis — after somewhat inappropriately naming the place "Bishop of Osnaberg's Island" — ordered sails to be set and a course was steered for a high island that the lookout had glimpsed in the west-south-west. And next morning, after a night of "dirty Squally weather," the early fog lifted to reveal lofty mountains laced with waterfalls, plantations lush with fruit-bearing trees — and a great fleet of canoes gathered about the ship.

The date was June 19, 1767, and "Otaheite" had been discovered by the first Europeans.

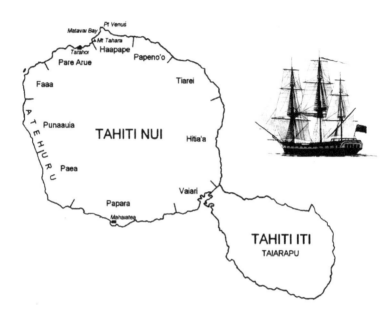

Map of old Tahiti © Ron Druett 2012

# Chapter 3:
## "A beauteous scene, to Britons new"

*In a short time the fogg cleard up, and we saw the E<sup>t</sup>*
*most point of this Land bearing N° two Leag<sup>s</sup>, at same*
*time saw breakers betwixt us and the shoar — and*
*upward of a hundred canoes betwixt us and the brakers*
*all paddling off towards the ship, when they came within*
*pistol shot they lay by for some time — and lookt at our*
*ship with great astonishment*

— Robertson, journal, *Dolphin*, June 19, 1767

"At 8 AM we got close in under the Island," wrote Wallis in his private journal; "when it clear'd away & we were surprized to find we were surrounded by some Hundred of Canoes, which had from One Man to ten in them who made such hallowing and Hooting that we could scarce hear each other speak." To his great relief, although the island was "very high in Peaks," the hillsides were cultivated, "full of Cocoa Nutt and fruit Trees, and from the Tops of the Mountains we saw large Rivers falling down into the Sea."

Obviously, the land was well inhabited, as not only could he see those well-tended plantations, but the beach was lined with houses — and then there was that great fleet of canoes. Wallis gave orders for the ship to be hauled aback, so that the *Dolphin* lay still, in invitation for visitors

— "we made signs for some of them to come onboard," he wrote. His sailing master, the large, jocular, and eloquent George Robertson, wrote at greater length, describing a scene where the men in the canoes lifted their paddles, and sat staring "with great astonishment," while their leaders held some kind of consultation. Trying to entice them closer, the *Dolphin* sailors who were fit enough to be on deck leaned over the rail, making "all the friendly signs that we could think of," dangling such enticements as strings of beads and ribbons in their scarred and tarry hands.

Finally the headsman stood up in the leading canoe, "and made signs of friendship to us, by holding up Branches of Plantain trees, and making a long speech of near fifteen minutes." Then he threw the sprout into the water.

Evidently this was a signal, as "one fine brisk young man" leaped into the mizzen chains, clambered lithely up the shrouds of the stern-most mast, and reached the wooden awning that shaded the quarterdeck. There he perched, laughing at the Europeans, who gathered at the bottom, beckoning and calling out. Finally, he jumped to the deck, accepted a few trinkets, and was shown how to shake hands, which he found even funnier.

Encouraged, a few friends threw peacemaking plantain shoots onto the deck, and then clambered up to join him. The young men were a fine sight — healthy, straight-limbed, golden brown, tall, and stalwart, Adonis types, all of them. Their broad, brown chests were bare, and their loins were covered with white breech-clouts, while their long black hair was tied up into topknots or trailed over muscular shoulders. Many had black designs on their legs, arms, and buttocks, which the Englishmen, being ignorant of tattoos, thought were painted.

They all had strong, white, even teeth, which they showed in very broad grins, particularly when the British sailors, desperate to convey their need for fresh food, "Grunted and Cryd lyke a Hogg, then pointed to the shore," as Robertson reminisced; while others crowed "Lyke cocks, to make them understand that we wanted fowls." To the relief of all, "this the natives of the country understood and Grunted and Crowd the same as our people, and pointed to the shore and made signs that they would bring us off some."

To everyone's surprise, what the natives wanted in exchange was iron, something Robertson learned when those on board "began to pull and hall at the Iron stanchions and Iron ring balls in order to carie them off." Hastily, the *Dolphin* seamen showed them nails, and though these were an acceptable substitute to start with, their visitors soon wanted more. Indeed, wrote Robertson, "they seemd very fond of everything which they saw made of Iron, and began to be unwilling to go out of the ship without some Iron work."

This was a bad development. Up to this moment life, for the *Dolphin*s, had seemed much more promising, with the warm sun blessing them all, and a fertile land beckoning beyond the ship's rail. The native men were friendly as well as good-looking, and seemed very willing to help out with fresh food. There had been much laughter, especially when the ship's goat had taken part in the fun, butting one of the islanders in the bottom. With one horrified look at the strange horned beast, the victim had sprung precipitately overboard, which amused them all.

But this obsession with iron signaled a change in mood. As Robertson noted, when they found that the ironwork was not easily prized away, the natives began to "be a Little surly."

37

The Europeans were getting agitated, too. Portable items were disappearing fast, handed down to the canoes before anyone could stop them. Though it was only natural that the natives should be fascinated by these new and exotic artifacts, nothing on the ship could be easily replaced.

"They are so thievish," complained Captain Wallis in his logbook, "that if they lay hands on anything they take it & Jump overboard immediately." When prevented from thieving, the natives became aggressive. In response to their shouts, the fleet paddled still closer, unmistakably menacing, so Furneaux ordered a cannon loaded with a nine-pound ball and aimed in the air directly above the canoes, "in order to frighten them in their Boats."

Up until the moment the cannon was fired, the natives on the deck had been watching the preparations with uncomprehending interest, but, as Robertson wrote, the explosion "hade the desird Effect." The shocked visitors dived overboard, though a particularly saucy fellow had enough presence of mind to snatch Midshipman Ibbott's gold-laced hat as he went. He recovered fast, too. Twenty yards off, he turned in the water, flourished the hat, and put it on his own head. The marines angrily pointed their muskets, but the youth did not understand. Instead, he laughed.

Emboldened by his example, the islanders were coming back, paddling vigorously to surround the ship. The seamen made sail, and the *Dolphin* fled to the open sea.

Once the canoes had given up the chase, Wallis was forced to turn back again. He had no choice. There was no way he could abandon any hope of re-provisioning his ship, so the *Dolphin* kept a course along the northern coast.

As the course became northwesterly, still following the shore, the officers began to wonder if this was an island and not the sought-for *Terra Australis Incognita*, the discovery of which would have brought them fame and some measure of fortune. However, even if it was just an island, it did promise everything else they needed — once they had found a friendly anchorage, where they could stay the four or five weeks necessary to recover their health and replenish the ship for the onward voyage.

Cautiously scudding along the coast, Wallis "saw a Large Canoe under sail in Shore – Breakers all along as we go – a great way of shore, the Land very Mountainous." Landing a boat was going to be difficult, but the attempt had to be made, so once the ship was abreast a likely gap in the reef, a boat was lowered with John Gore in charge, and sent into the lagoon.

Canoes came out to parley, and with pleasure Wallis saw through his spyglass that they were loaded with coconuts, plantains, and pigs, evidently to exchange for nails. So perhaps, he thought, trading could be made safely from the boats, but then to his alarm he saw that Gore's boat had become surrounded by "a vast Number of Canoes full of people" who were throwing stones and shouting what were obviously threats.

Hastily, he "made the Signal to come on board," by firing another nine-pound shot. This did the trick, and half an hour later the boat was back, but Gore's report was not at all promising. Not only was the lagoon too deep for an anchorage — "they could not get ground with 70 fath. Line" — but the boat had been menaced by about a hundred canoes.

There were warriors on board with slingshots, and when the first hail of stones had stormed over the boat, Gore had fired a musket into the air to warn them away.

This had triggered a great shout from the paddlers — of challenge, not alarm, for the canoes had merely forged closer. So Gore had taken aim and fired another shot, deliberately wounding one of the natives in his throwing arm.

And so the first Tahitian experienced the full impact of European firepower.

The boat's retreat had been hazardous altogether, Robertson recording that the canoes "Endeavord to cut him off from the ship but the cutter being a fine clean Boat saild faster nor they could paddle, and non of them had sails." Though Gore and his men had made it safely back on board the ship, more than a few had suffered cuts and bruises from the flung stones. It was time to give up on this part of the coast, and try again somewhere to the west.

Wallis gave the order to make sail again, but then a large double canoe was seen approaching the ship. Hoping that there was a man of importance, like a chief — or even a native king — on board, Wallis recanted the order and waited for the canoe to approach.

"She appeard to sail very fast and soon got along side," wrote Robertson. One of the occupants threw a plantain branch onto the deck, which by now they all recognized as a peacemaking gesture, "and the Capt Gave him some toys which seemd to pleas him much."

Ominously, however, the young man flaunting the midshipman's gilt-braided hat was on board the canoe, and again the encounter ended in chaos.

As Wallis noted in the logbook, "we had some hundreds of Canoes about the Ship – to whom I gave Nails & some trifles but they brought nothing in exchange & so thievish that they were clambering up the Side & taking everything they could lay hands on." So, after chasing the natives away, the *Dolphin* made sail in earnest, and kept on her course, heading still further northwest along the coast.

Frustratingly, the late afternoon sun gleamed on a vista that "the most Beautiful appearance its posable to Imagin," as Robertson wrote. All along the coast the hillsides were marked with well-tended plantations, and the beaches were lined with houses, "all very neatly thatched, with Great Numbers of Cocoa Nut Trees," while the mountains that loomed above were rifted with beautiful valleys.

Robertson guessed that the population was enormous, as the beaches were lined with hordes of men and women, gazing raptly as the ship passed by. None, however, pushed out their canoes to investigate, and when several very large double canoes came out of the sea to the northwest, the massive craft made no attempt to come near the ship. Instead, they sailed on regardless, skimming the water at a great rate, Robertson estimating with some awe that they could sail at least one fourth faster than the *Dolphin*.

At sunset, a promising bay was sighted, so the ship lay off and on outside the reef all night, making short tacks back and forth to keep more or less in the same place, ready for going in at dawn. This time, two boats were lowered, one commanded by Gore and the other by Robertson. Both were crammed with well-armed, exceedingly nervous men.

As they pulled away from the ship great numbers of canoes could be seen setting out from the beach. When they came up with the two boats, the men in the canoes angrily waved Gore and Robertson away, but it was impossible to concede, as the situation on board was so desperate. Both the captain and the first lieutenant were too ill to get out of their berths. Several seamen were close to death. Gore and Robertson ignored the islanders' warnings, sending a signal to the *Dolphin* that a safe harbor had been found. The ship entered the gap in the reef and anchored two miles from the shore.

After getting back to the ship, the two boats were hoisted on board, and for a long time the *Dolphin*s waited to see what the natives would do. Slowly and hesitantly, one canoe came out to the ship, and then others followed, loaded with coconuts, fruit, a few fowls, and some pigs. The islanders proved to be sharp traders, refusing to hand over their bananas and pigs until they had received their nails, often demanding more than the previously agreed number. Fists were lifted as their demeanor became increasingly insulting, but at last the ship had a supply of fresh food.

Drinking water was another priority. The ship carried a distilling apparatus, made up of a big copper cauldron where seawater was boiled, with pipes which condensed the steam into drinking water. It was controlled by the very competent surgeon, John Hutchinson, who was apt to boast he could make forty-two gallons of fresh water from fifty-six gallons of seawater in one four-hour watch — but for that he needed fuel, and there was very little firewood, so the apparatus was idle. The boats were put out again, and Robertson and Gore were sent off to search for a suitable stream.

By the time they were in the surf, which was running high, they were surrounded by a hundred-strong fleet, including double-hulled sailing canoes. The men inside them hooted in challenge. Thousands of yelling people thronged the beach, many contemptuously beckoning, daring the men to come on shore.

Outnumbered and intimidated, Robertson and Gore decided to retreat, but found they had left it too late.

Before they were a third of the way to the ship, both boats were attacked. The double canoes racing up to them were equipped with fighting platforms on the foredecks, where warriors armed with clubs were standing ready for combat. Gore's men fought back, hacking and stabbing with their bayonets, and managed to beat off their attackers. George Robertson, however, was forced to order his marines to fire their guns.

Two natives fell into the water, one dead, and the other mortally wounded. Their companions dived overboard and hoisted them back into the canoe. Then, with growing puzzlement, they tried to make the dead man stand or sit up. By the time the natives had worked out that somehow, mysteriously, he had been killed from a distance by the stick that spat fire, Robertson's boat had escaped.

For a while it looked as if the islanders had learned their lesson. Next day, when canoes came out to the ship to trade, thieving or cheating was swiftly stopped by pointing a musket or even a spyglass at the offender. The natives were intelligent, obviously, as they already understood how their fellows had been killed — as Robertson wrote, "They calld loudly bon-bon, then smate their breasts and forehead and laid backward with their eyes fixd and without motion."

A payment system had been established, too: a 20-pound hog was worth a twenty-penny (four-inch) nail, while a suckling pig was worth a 10-penny (three-inch) nail, and a fowl could be bought with a sixpenny nail, a spike just two inches long. Robertson remarked that a string of beads would buy a hen or a bunch of fruit, "but all of them seemd most fond of nails."

The surf was still too high for the seamen to go on shore and find fresh water, so the following day natives were bribed with nails to fill some barrels and bring them to the boats. However, two of the irreplaceable kegs were stolen. When Robertson and Gore demanded their return, the islanders merely smirked, and brought a bevy of attractive young girls, instead.

The girls pulled up their thigh-length sarongs to reveal the nakedness underneath, and "made a thousand antick tricks to entice them on land," as Wallis wrote in his logbook, after hearing about it. The native men laughed merrily at the sailors' half-scandalized, half-fascinated reaction, and when the boats beat a prudent retreat, the women disdainfully pelted them with fruit and stones, making it plain that they thought them impotent.

The next day, another attempt was made to get fresh water, but again the casks were stolen, and again the girls teased and tormented the sailors. It was an impossible situation, as not only were the natives uncooperative in the extreme, but they were becoming "greatly inraged against us." Two had already been killed, and more were going to die if the *Dolphin* lingered any longer.

Accordingly, the anchor was raised, and the sails set. The decision had been made to try to find a more hospitable anchorage, by coasting still farther west.

And so the *Dolphin* arrived at Matavai Bay.


They called it Port Royal. It was the most promising anchorage yet, with a large, tranquil lagoon between the reef and the beach, surrounded by forested hills. On the foreshore, a thatched longhouse was set among coconut palms and fruit-bearing trees. Canoes were drawn up on the beach before it, but there was no scurry to push them into the water and prevent the *Dolphin* from coming inside the reef.

Instead, it was an accident that nearly wrecked her.

When the ship was working her way through the gap, she struck a rock, became pinned at the bow, and was stranded there for about an hour. When the natives saw the Europeans' predicament, hundreds of canoes came off from shore, and paddled about her, anticipating the pillage that would follow the wreck. But, to the great relief of all on board, a favorable breeze sprang up and filled the *Dolphin*'s sails, and the ship's head swung off the rock.

A second attempt at sailing through the passage was successful, and a fine mooring place beckoned, abreast of a stream of water running to the left of a high promontory that was crowned by a single tree. Dark was falling, but at dawn the seamen could easily warp her inshore, by taking out anchors in the ship's boats, dropping them into the water ahead, and hauling the ship up to the anchors with the windlass.

As the sun went down, most of the canoes returned to the beach, but several remained, some restlessly circling the ship. The island became shrouded with shadows, so it was impossible to see what was happening on the beach. Nervewrackingly, as night fell, the dark was punctuated by a multitude of flickering lights on the reef. The men on watch were issued cutlasses and pistols, and the gun crews assembled.

And so the nervous hours wore on.

*Matavai Bay, from "Skirmish Hill," and with canoes,*
*from Hawkesworth's Voyages V.II*

# Chapter 4:
## "And deem our floating world a prize"

*At sun rise about three hundred canoes came off and*
*lay round the ship, as many as could conveniently lay*
*alongside traded very fair and took nails and Toys for*
*their Hogs, fowls and fruit, but Eight o'clock their was*
*upwards of five hundred canoes round the ship, and at a*
*Moderate Computation there was near four thousand*
*men*
— Robertson, journal, *Dolphin,* June 24, 1767

At sunrise, all seemed peaceful. After breakfast had
been eaten, the seamen started working the ship up to the
chosen anchorage. Captain Wallis was confined to his
cabin, being more sick than ever with his bilious fever, but
the competent Furneaux was in charge.

Everything seemed to be going well, the ship echoing to
the normal shouts of men at work, but when Wallis went
to the quarter gallery that ran off the stern cabin, he looked
out the window to see that the *Dolphin* was completely
surrounded by canoes. There were over three hundred, or
so he estimated, and more were coming all the time.
Ominously, too, the beaches were crowded with thousands of people, who behaved like spectators who were
awaiting some spectacle to come.

Wallis had already ordered that the guns and muskets
were loaded. The seamen were armed with cutlasses and

pistols. At all times thirty armed marines were stationed along the rails, looking out for trouble, but still there was a great sense of impending danger. But then, as he tensely studied the nearest canoes, he saw that they were loaded deep with pigs, fowls, and fruit. It looked as if trading would go on in the old fashion, with the natives haggling shrewdly for their nails, and the sailors watching them narrowly to forestall any attempt at cheating or theft. And it seemed successful, too, as the trading was going on fairly, with no trouble at all, and the more fresh food that came on board for the men in the sickbay, the better.

And so Captain Wallis relaxed.

Suspicions were lulled, but nevertheless he stayed in the gallery to keep watch. Another wave of canoes came up to the side of the ship, but this time the load was different. Naked girls rose like nymphs from the middle of the thwarts, and, as drums rattled out a fast, seductive beat, they set to "making all the Lascivious Motions, & playing all the wanton tricks imaginable." Lithe hips whirled and gyrated, feet and knees tapped, and slender arms undulated,  as young, sensuous bodies kept time to the fast, provocative rhythm.

Amazed and titillated, the British seamen abandoned their work, dropping muskets and tools to clamber onto the bulwarks and into the rigging, where they could get a better view. While they were raptly staring, still more canoes slid near — large double canoes, crewed by men who, according to Wallis at the gallery windows, were blowing conches, playing flutes, and singing hoarsely, "& I perceived they had vast Quantities of Pebble Stones of a Pound to two & three weight."

On deck, Robertson also "observed great numbers of stones in every canoe." But, when he talked it over with shipmates who had also noticed this, they decided it was not worth worrying about, as brisk trading was still going on, "and all the men seemed as hearty and merry as the girls."

Captain Wallis, in the quarter gallery, also decided that the stones were there as ballast, to balance the big canoes, but still he felt suspicious enough to send for Lieutenant Furneaux, and order him to have gun crews stationed by the two quarterdeck cannon. Then he, like Robertson on deck, turned his attention to the elaborately caparisoned canoe with two tall, carved sterns that sailed at the head of the oncoming fleet.

This, like the *Dolphin*, had a big wooden canopy, and an imposing figure was perched cross-legged on this, almost level with the deck of the ship. His turbaned head was wreathed with leaves and flowers, and he had more garlands about his neck. His robes were pristine white, and he was holding a plantain shoot high in one hand, while he clasped a "Bunch of various coloured feathers" in the other.

The green branch was waved in what Wallis perceived as a peacemaking gesture. Then, with his other hand — the one holding the feathers — this commanding figure pointed first at his own chest, and then at the ship.

So, Wallis thought, a man of great significance had at last come to visit — a chief! Perhaps even a king, come to formalize the precarious situation, a man with whom he could negotiate trading arrangements, and make a treaty for annexation of the island.

George Robertson, on deck, came to exactly the same conclusion. This great carved canoe had "several of the Principle Inhabitance in her," as he wrote, adding, "we afterwards found out that the King of the Island and several of the Grandees was in this canoe."

Leaning out of the window, Captain Wallis politely gestured for the "king" to come on board. But, to his great surprise, instead of rising from the canopy the white-robed potentate passed the bunch of feathers to a seaman, and with an imperious gesture commanded him to carry it to his leader.

Still puzzled, Wallis went to the door of the Great Cabin to receive the tuft of bright feathers — with no idea that it was a 'ura-tatae, a fetish meant to focus the malign attention of the gods onto the ship — and after taking it back into the cabin, he occupied himself in "preparing some presents" to be given to the chief in return for the pretty object. And then he became aware that a deathly silence had fallen on the waters outside.

On deck, the seamen saw the ceremonial canoe paddle some distance away, then come to a stop. Slowly and momentously, the chief on the awning drew a red mantle about his shoulders, picked up a staff that lay before him, and thrust it high in the air.

It was a signal. With a universal shout hundreds of warriors leaped onto the fighting platforms of the bigger canoes, which charged the ship, while the trading canoes backed off quickly, to make way.

A hail of stones hammered through the rigging of the *Dolphin*, and crashed onto the decks. Seamen tumbled down from where they were exposed in the bulwarks and rigging, many bruised and bleeding. The sergeant bawled an order, and the marines leveled their muskets. The snap and rattle of a volley was answered by more warlike shouting from the native men, who "powerd in the stones lyke hail amongst us which hurt a great many of our men," wrote Robertson. "We then found lenity would not do, therefor applied to the Great Guns."

Panicked orders were bawled, and the snouts of the two quarterdeck guns were run out. A roar of, "Fire!" Powder exploded. With a grumble of wheels the cannon bounced back against their ropes. Stinging smoke billowed, and the air rang with the double concussion.

The surface of the lagoon became the stuff of nightmare. The two cannon had been armed with grapeshot — bags of small iron balls, which burst apart when fired, scattering their lethal load. These were not warning shots, but deliberately aimed at boats and people, the murderous impact of which, as Robertson wrote, "struck such terror amongs the poor unhappy croad that it would require the pen of Milton to describe, therefor too mutch for mine."

As Wallis recorded later in self-justification, "I believe there was not less than three Hundred Boats about the Ship, and on an average Two Thousand Men, besides some Thousands on the Shore and boats coming from every quarter."

Five hundred yards away, double canoes gathered about the ceremonial craft, as if for an urgent conference with their "king." A long, fraught pause, while the *Dolphin*s reloaded their cannon, and then waited to see what would happen next. The surgeon, John Hutchinson, and his mate, Robert Saunderson, moved about the decks, binding up the cuts and bruises of those who had been hit by stones, but there were none gravely wounded, and no British dead.

"Saw an Indian Woman floating athwart our cut-water, having received a Shot in her Belly," wrote one of the young midshipmen, George Pinnock.

Hoisting white streamers, the big canoes made another dash for the *Dolphin*, the warriors on the fighting platforms hurling stones from slingshots as they came. The ship was heaved around so her broadside bore down on them, and a

51

hail of iron seared the oncoming fleet, aimed directly at the admiral's canoe. Shouted orders, two more deafening explosions. The ship rocked with the concussion.

When the smoke cleared, the canoes were beating a panic-stricken retreat to the beach. Incredibly, however, still more war canoes were joining the fleet, dragged down from the beach and shoved into the water, where they gathered about the "king's canoe" for another council of war. As Robertson observed, in their innocence they thought themselves out of range of the guns. More orders were bellowed, and this time, the guns were aimed directly at the ceremonial canoe, where, as the *Dolphins* believed, the "king" was rallying his forces.

And again a hail of iron stormed over the water.

Wrote Robertson, "we resolved to prevent him and his friends in the Boat, from Attempting any such thing again, therefor pointed two Great Guns at this Great Canoe well loaded with round and Grape shot, which soon drove her in two and I believe few that was in her Escaped with life."

To his amazement, a handful of brave men hung back to salvage the two pieces of the chief's craft, and carry its wounded and dead away — "they behaved so brave, that they not only cared off the Lame and Dead Men, but they even towed off the two shaterd ends of the canoe to the end of a reeff." A shot was fired at them, but even this "did not make this handful of Brave men give over their good offices to their chiefs."

And still the war canoes came — three hundred more, according to Robertson's estimation. The destruction became even more deliberate, the officers waiting until the fleet was within three or four hundred yards of the ship before ordering the gun crews to fire.

Again and again the appalling blast of a broadside crashed out, tearing the new fleet apart, to be followed by another and yet another, this time aimed at the thousands of people who packed the beaches. When the guns silenced, the bay echoed with screams of pain and fear. Bodies floated past the *Dolphin*, caught in reddened eddies.

On shore, the people were fleeing for the hills and disappearing in the trees. Then they were gone. "At Noon," George Robertson wrote, "there was not one canoe to be seen in the Water, nor ten people to be seen all along shore."

The sun was high in the sky, and the waters of the bay were as empty as the bloodstained beaches.

"A representation of the attack of Captain Wallis in the Dolphin by the natives of Otaheite," from Hawkesworth's *Voyages*

Ceremonial canoe, from Ellis, *Polynesian Voyages* (1782)

# Chapter 5:
# "In George's royal name"

*Fine pleasant weather, at 3 PM sent Liu. Furneaux with Sixty Men Armed to the Shoar to find out a Watering Place and take Possession by right of Conquest in the Name & for the use of his most Sacred Majesty King George the 3: and of the other Island to the Westward* (Moorea) *in the Name of his Royal Highness the Duke of York*

— Wallis's logbook, *Dolphin*, June 26, 1767

Three hours passed. Since the natives had fled, the men had been busy, warping the ship up to the watering place, anchoring her well, and bringing more cannon up from the hold. Everyone was nervous, expecting another attack, probably in the night, but for now the *Dolphin* sat quietly on top of her reflection in the mid-afternoon sun.

Hesitantly, a few canoes came out to trade, "with Green Boughs and Plantain leaves as emblems of Peace," wrote Robertson, "but we Suffer'd very few of them to come near the Ship, and those that we permitted seemed very much terrified."

One of the men took advantage of this, by paying for a fowl with a blow of his fist, instead of the agreed-upon nail, and was flogged for it, somewhat to the stupefaction of the natives involved. Wallis then ordered that only the officers should conduct trade, saying that he did not trust the men.

It was also time to take formal possession of the island, though he very much regretted that it had had to be done by force. So Lieutenant Furneaux, still being the only deck officer fit enough, was sent the beach with three boats, eighteen seamen, three midshipmen, a marine sergeant, and twelve marines.

Every man was armed. Because of the gravity of the occasion, Furneaux wore his best uniform — a splendid blue coat, white silk breeches, and a gold-buttoned cocked hat. The sun glittered on his gold decorations as the boats were rowed to the nearer side of the river. Thousands of natives watched, having silently assembled on the other side of the water. So many of the Tahitians held peacemaking plantain fronds high that the crowd looked like a human forest, but the boats were kept afloat in four feet of water, prepared for a quick getaway if necessary. Molyneux, in charge, had a heavy musketoon ready loaded and aimed. The atmosphere, on both sides, was fraught.

There was a time-honored routine to this British annexing of a newly discovered territory. The marine squad lined up on the beach, and carried out an exercise, presenting arms with a stamp, and snapping the muskets down again, while the Tahitians watched, impressed. Then Lieutenant Tobias Furneaux made signs for a representative to come over and parley.

There was a pause as a messenger was sent to the top of the hill, and then an old man arrived. Fearfully, he crossed the river. He was carrying a plantain shoot and a small pig, and was accompanied by two equally elderly friends. Talking volubly and unintelligibly, he laid down the pig, and put the branch on top of it. Furneaux, after an incomprehensible speech of his own, gave the old man some nails and "toys," such as beads and ribbons. He then asked for water, and the old fellow, understanding at once, waved an arm, inviting them to take as much as he wanted. While a few seamen filled a couple of casks at the clear, fresh river, another sailor turned a sod and planted a tall stick in the soil of Tahiti.

A solemn, portentous ritual commenced, one that all the Tahitians watched intently, because to all appearances it was carried out in honor of some invisible, powerful god. The brilliantly uniformed Furneaux produced and flourished a document that Captain Wallis had penned, and in sonorous tones renamed Tahiti "King George the Third Island," proclaiming it a British possession. The ship's pennant was ceremoniously hoisted up the tall stick, and the marines fired a simultaneous musket salute. A toast of brandy mixed with good Tahitian river water was drunk, and three hearty cheers were roared from British throats. Birds wheeled high in the sky like shadows of the offended gods, and the massed Tahitians trembled.

Though the *Dolphin*s had not noticed it, the islanders had become very disturbed. When several men came across the river with offerings of pigs, fruit, and plantain sprouts, and hastened back without waiting for payment, Furneaux merely assumed a good supply of provisions was now guaranteed. After leaving some nails and two billhooks on the sand, he shook hands with the old man, and led his marines and sailors away, feeling very pleased with himself. It was not until he was back on board that he began to take note of the Tahitians' strange reaction to the flag.

George Robertson, likewise, was mystified when, through his spyglass, he saw the old man and one of his friends approach the flag "with as much ceremony as if it had been a Demi God." From the decks of the ship, he and the other *Dolphins* watched the two old men fall onto their knees and appear to pray. Puzzled, they hunted for a reason, with no idea that the long, red, triangular pennant was the same shape and color as one of the Tahitians' most sacred icons, the *maro 'ura*, a red-feathered loincloth that had demanded hundreds of human sacrifices in its making, and was regarded with reverent dread. After casting some green boughs at its foot, the two old men crossed the river, to return with a dozen men, all carrying plantain shoots, who humbly crept toward the flag, taking one slow step after another. The wind gusted, and it flapped with a crack like thunder. Terrified, they ran off.

When a handful of islanders were brave enough to come back, they were bearing two large live hogs. These were laid down at the foot of the staff, as if in propitiation. The pennant hung still, so after some praying and dancing they carried the hogs to a beached canoe. The old man and one of his friends clambered inside, and paddled to the side of the ship. There, visibly trembling, he stood and made a long speech. Finishing at last, he presented the foreigners with several plantain shoots and then the two large pigs, gesturing at the pennant all the time. Then, after refusing to accept anything in return, or come on board, the two Tahitians hurriedly paddled away.

More mystified than ever, the *Dolphins* watched the two old men arrive at the beach, abandon the canoe, and scurry across the river. They disappeared into the trees, and then there was silence. All the people were gone; it was as if the island were deserted. The sailors on the *Dolphin* waited, but nothing from shore was to be seen or heard. The sun set in a tropical blaze of purple, gold, and red. Then, as night fell, there was movement.

"At night we heard the noise of Many Conchs, Drums and wind instruments," remembered Captain Wallis. And a multitude of lights progressed towards them along the coast.

Closer they came, closer, the torch-fires blowing in the wind, the chanting and drumming growing louder and louder. Scared by the solemnity of the procession, the *Dolphin*s thought the Tahitians were bringing firebrands to burn the ship. Two three-pounder cannon were set on the forecastle, facing the beach with its parade of lights, and each was loaded with a bag of seventy musket balls. But still there was no attack.

And so the nervous night wore on.

*Detail from sketch by Captain Wallis, National Library of Australia*

When dawn broke there were no canoes in the water. The beaches were as deserted as the lagoon. Everything looked just as it had the afternoon before.

Except that the red pennant had been taken away.

*At 6 AM [June 26] sent Lieu[t] Furneaux with Sixty Men to fill water & endeavor to get a trade for Provision and fruit with the Natives in Exchange for Hatchetts beads &c – at ½ past 7 got off three Tons of Water, at 8 a great Number of the Inhabitants appeared from amongst the trees each side of the River, and approached our people that was on the Beach, who made them signs to keep at a distance*

—Wallis, logbook, *Dolphin*, June 26, 1767

Having formally annexed the island, the priority was to load with fresh water. Captain Wallis was still too weak to stand unsupported, and the first lieutenant, William Clarke, was confined to his sickbed as well, so again Furneaux was the only officer fit enough to take command of a shore party. As before, George Robertson was left in charge of the ship.

One by one, the barge, cutter, and launch were hoisted up from the skids amidships, and lowered onto the water, where they lay bouncing as sixty men jumped down into them, many of them armed marines. No canoes arrived to prevent the party from landing, and no one materialized from the groves of trees to receive them on the beach. To all appearances the old man, with all his companions, had vanished from the face of the earth. Lulled by the quietness of the morning, Furneaux reported back at the ship that all was well, and the watering process began.

Empty casks were pushed over the gangway in a series of splashes, then were attached by the boatmen to long ropes, and towed behind the boats like clustered beads on a string. At the beach, the barrels were trundled to the river, and pushed underwater with their open bung holes uppermost. After they had filled and sunk, the bungs were rammed hard home, and the casks, much heavier now, were rolled to the boats, and attached again to the towlines. Back at the side of the *Dolphin*, they were laboriously muscled up over the rail and down into the hold, using the mainyard as a hoist.

The work went smoothly. On shore, the dawning sun gleamed on glossy leaves and wave-rippled sand, a scented breeze wafted down from the hills, and birds sang in the trees. The warm air echoed with the gurgle of filling casks, the chuckle of the river, the casual voices of the seamen, the crunch of sand beneath their bare feet, and the suck and rush of breakers on the distant reef.

Then the air was split by warning shrieks from the lookouts aloft. A fleet of canoes was approaching from the southwest point of the bay, and on shore a thousand-strong procession was winding down from the top of the hill to where the barrels were being filled.

As Robertson recorded, "we observed a great number of large canoes, coming towards the ship from the S.W. side of the Bay, and all full of men, at the same time we saw several thousands of Men comeing along shore toward the River, the first great body of men came over the top of a Hill in the Bottom of the Bay, with our pendant flying at the end of a long pole."

Naturally, Captain Wallis expected another skirmish: "we saw from the ships mast Crowds of People coming over the Hills, from every way seeming great haste," he recorded; "and severall hundred canoes came around a Point about a mile from the Ship, being full of Men, and from a Creek to the Eastward, a great Number More."

When the lookout reported canoes making directly for the watering boats, he "made the Signals for the Boats to come which they did immediately leaving the Casks behind them."

This led to panic at the *Dolphins'* side of the river. A fleet of about fifty canoes was advancing, and a flood of people was descending from the top of the hill. As they retreated, a small crowd rushed forward to seize the casks, and, seeing this, Wallis "Ordered a Shot to be fired at them and a few more at the Canoes," which beat a rapid retreat to the beach, where they hauled up their craft.

Wallis was not prepared to wait and see what they would do next. Instead, he ordered that the guns be aimed at the woods, "and some at a tree I believe a Mile & half Distance on a very high Hill where there were some Thousands assembled who had ran from the watering Place & from the Woods, two shot fell a little beyond the Tree and they all marched off."

Then, in an act of mindless destruction, he ordered Furneaux to carry the carpenters, with eighty men, on shore to destroy all the canoes they could reach — "he reported that many of them were Double & many in the Skirts of the Woods ready for Launching that we could not see," Wallis wrote on, in self-justification. Many were loaded with "great Quantities of large Pebbles of two or Three Pounds weight, several of the Canoes were fifty & sixty feet long, they had no Stock in & from the preparations they had made and their actions this morning I am firmly of opinion that they were bent on a second attack — had we not proceeded thus."

Naturally, the Tahitian men did their best to stop this mindless vandalism — "several of them venterd down through the wood, I suppose with an intention to prevent our men from disableing their canoes," wrote Robertson, "but the Gard which landed to protect the carpenters, fired upon them and soon put them to the flight — and obliged them to Retire to the top of Skirmish Hill." If they thought they were out of range there, the *Dolphin*s soon taught them otherwise, by sending a round shot skipping along the top of the hill — something, or so Robertson thought, that frightened them more than any of the other nightmares up to then.

Not only had the watering party escaped easily, but the savage revenge was pointless. Many of the beautiful craft that were so methodically destroyed had great ceremonial significance. As one of the seamen, John Nicholls, described, "two in particular were of a larger size than common, with very pretty carved work on them, much resembling the Doric Order of Architecture."

Altogether, it was a cruel, deliberate assault on Tahitian pride. These canoes had taken thousands of hours in their creation, from the careful selection of trees to the ceremonial of launching, every stage of which was blessed by priests. Apart from its psychological effect, the vandalism achieved nothing, since the *Dolphin*s knew very well it was impossible to destroy every canoe in Tahiti. They could even see a dozen large canoes getting under sail beyond the point, on the verge of escape.

And, though the Englishmen could not possibly know it, they were witnessing the terrified flight of a high chief, Amo, who had witnessed the destruction and slaughter, and his high priest and advisor, Tupaia — who was the man who had appropriated the red pennant.

*The instant the our Boat returnd from disableing all the canoes at the N. end of Skirmish Hill, we saw a large body of Men and Women Assembling on the beach to the Northward of the Watering place, and Bringing down Green boughs with Hogs pigs fowls and fruits, and a great quantity of White cloath, we supposed this people wanted to make peace with us, and what they were bringing down was intended for a peace offering to prevent us from destroying their canoes as we did those to the southward of the watering place*

*Immediately after dinner the seco<sup>d</sup> Lieu<sup>t</sup> took the Barge and Cutter Mand and Armd and the Launch Loaded with Empty Water Casks, he first brou<sup>t</sup> the Launch to an Anchor off the watering place, then Landed where the Peace Offering was laid down, and walkt a few steps towards the place where their canoes was halld up on the Beach, as if he meant to destroy them as he did those to the s'ward — when the natives saw him going towards the canoes they seemd Greatly afraid, and made all the signs of friendly that they could think of and pointed to the peace offering*

— Robertson, journal, *Dolphin*, June 27, 1769

# Chapter 6:
# "The girls well-featur'd, passing fair,
# And kind in all respects"

*... gave the Hogs that we got yesterday to the ships
Company which came to more than a Pound a Man,
made Broth of it which was very good, gave leave to the
People to take as many Cocoanutts that we brought from
Qu. Charlotts Island, & got of here the first day of
Anchoring at this Island as they could make use of
without waste*

— Wallis, logbook, *Dolphin*, June 26, 1767

At two in the afternoon, the Tahitians, having recognized defeat, embarked on the traditional peace-making ritual that ceremoniously followed a loss in tribal warfare, and was designed to appease the victors and tame their powers. To them, the time-worn ceremony was logical and correct; for the *Dolphins*, it was completely baffling.

As Wallis wrote, "at 2 PM about Ten of the Natives came down to the Beach with green boughs & stuck them up and then went back & returned with severall Hogs & Dogs tyed by the feet and laid them on the Beach & then they brought a Quantity of the Cloth that they Cloth themselves with & Hollered to us to come & receive it."

Understanding the gestures, if not the words, Captain Wallis sent Furneaux on shore, and to his satisfaction, he saw the natives retreat as the lieutenant's boat arrived, leaving him to collect the ceremonious offering.

But instead of politely receiving it all, and carrying it back to the ship, as the natives fully expected, Furneaux released the dogs — a culinary treat when cooked, and eaten only by men of the highest status — and set them loose. Then, after ordering his men to put the pigs, chickens, and fruit in the boats, he left nails and iron tools in exchange, and returned to the ship — abandoning the six great bundles of white cloth, leaving them lying forlornly on the sand. Yet, in the minds of the Tahitians, the acceptance of the sacred gift of tapa —"the breath of the gods" — was an essential part of the peacemaking rite.

The manufacture of tapa was a labor-intensive process, involving the whole community. The men's work was the careful planting and cultivation of paper mulberry trees. When the stems were about one inch thick, the bark was stripped from the saplings, soaked in a running stream, and then scraped, beaten, and flattened forcibly again by teams of women with tapa beaters, resulting in lengths of thin cloth about a yard wide, which could be more than thirty feet long. Often, these lengths were joined side by side, by pasting and more beating, resulting in broader fathoms. The final result was bleached to a luminous white, and the very best cloth was dyed.

Because it represented the strength, spirit, and enterprise of the entire village, fine tapa was the supreme gift, reserved for momentous occasions and the most important guests. In the truce-making ritual, by making a ceremonial presentation of tapa, the supplicant people acknowledged the superior might of the victors. When that tapa was accepted, the power of the recipients was symbolically captured. But the Europeans had spurned this significant gift, along with everything it symbolized.

Furneaux was not a stupid or imperceptive man. After he got back to the ship, he noticed that the Tahitians were milling about in agitation, and belatedly realized he had blundered in leaving the cloth, which the ship did not need, and which he had thought the natives could not easily spare.

Much to the relief of the local people, the boats returned to the beach and the bundles were collected — "and they went away rejoicing," as Wallis wrote, allowing the Europeans to collect more fresh water.

Still, the only intermediary was the white-bearded elder, consistently called "the Old Man," but whose name, as later Europeans found, was Fa'a. Doing his best to communicate the Englishmen's fear that there would be another attack, Furneaux took Fa'a to where stones were piled along the side of the river, and indicated that these were the source of trouble. And so, as Wallis described, "the Old Man turned round to his People & shewd the Stones & spoke to them & shook his head, pointing at the ship, many of the people went away & returned with Yams Plantains & Bread fruit a few fowles & Roasting Pigs."

As always, the lieutenant was meticulous about paying for these with nails and tools. The result was that so much produce was brought to the beach that Captain Wallis was able to record that Furneaux returned on board at sunset, "with fresh Provisions enough for the Ships Company, and the Surgeon being of Opinion that giving the Company a Breakfast of Wheat, Bread fruit, Bananas & Apples would be of great assistance to them in clearing them of scorbutic complaint."

*... an Old Man that had been over at the watering place, come from the side where the natives were to our People & exchanged Hogs Apples &c for knives, beads, Nails & other things — so that we have plenty of fresh Provisions & fruit*

— Wallis, logbook, *Dolphin*, June 28, 1767

At last, as the natives continued their peacemaking gestures, and the trading went on apace, Wallis felt secure enough to allow the surgeon to take the sick men on shore, and set them up in tents. Naturally, marines went with them, to keep sentry duty, and as it was a convenient place for trading, the gunner, William Harrison, was sent ashore too, to set up a trading tent.

Wallis made sure this was well regulated — "the Gunner had Orders not to Suffer any to Straggle or Trade with the Natives but himself, to whom I gave Cloth, Beads, Knives, Buttons, Scissors, Nails, and many other things he returned at Night with Twenty small Hogs, some fowles, Breadfruit, Bananas & Apples."

But, while Harrison was doing very well, he was under difficulties — as was Fa'a. Being the only Tahitian allowed to cross the river, the old man had to deal with all the pe`ople who had brought goods to trade, and then carry over the foodstuffs himself. Sometimes he was allowed to requisition a friend to help, usually a young man who was supposed by the *Dolphin*s to be his son, but this made little difference.

Not only did it greatly reduce the amount of foodstuffs traded, but it meant that the local nobility had no chance to approach the Europeans. They gathered on the far side of the river with their ceremonial stools and servants, eager to parley, but Harrison had strict orders not to allow them to cross. Instead, he ordered the guard to threaten them with muskets if they so much as put a foot in the water, which was not only an unprecedented insult, but also very frightening.

The other problem was the men themselves. It was easy enough to prevent the natives from coming over the river, but the men were a different matter — and this included the ambulatory sick, as well as the marines on guard and the seamen who were assisting Harrison. Naturally, having recovered their strength after months at sea, the men were lusty, and the girls were indeed very beautiful.

On the day that Furneaux went back to the beach to pick up the tapa cloth, Robertson recorded with tongue-in-cheek amusement that the second lieutenant's boat's crew had been very tempted by the girls on display — "our Young men seeing several very handsome Young girls, they could not help feasting their Eyes with so agreeable a sight."

As he went on to describe, Fa'a and the other old men saw this as another way of making peace, and "made them stand in Rank, and made signs for our people to take which they liked best, and as many as they liked, and for fear our men hade been Ignorant and not known how to use the poor young Girls, the old men made signs how we should behave to the Young women, this all the boats crew seemd to understand perfectly well, and begd the Officer would receive a few of the Young Woman onboard."

The officer, Furneaux, who knew perfectly well what Captain Wallis's reaction would be if he were silly enough to take girls back to the ship, refused the request, but, once back on board, his boat's crew wasted no time at all in telling the rest of the seamen about the girls — "swore they neaver saw handsomer made women in their lives, and declard they would all to a man, live on two thirds allowance, rather nor lose so fine an opportunity of getting a Girl apiece — this piece of news made all our men madly fond of the shore, even the sick which hade been on the doctors list for some weeks before, now declard they would be happy if they were permited to go ashore, at the same time said a Young Girl would make an Excelent Nurse, and they were Certain of recovering faster under a Young Girls care nor all the doctor would do for them." And so they "past this Night very merry supposing all hostilitys was now over and," he added, "to our great joy it so happened."

It was inevitable that the men, even those in the sick tents, would defy orders, and "straggle" into the trees. Wallis noted disapprovingly in his private log, "the Women particularly fond of prostituting themselves," but, being pragmatic, and a seaman himself, he did not try to stop the trade knowing that any effort would be useless. Instead, he advised the men to keep on their guard. However, that was not necessary, either, as Robertson was right, and all hostilities had ended.

In the beginning, the trade in sex was not just simple prostitution. Instead, it was the well-intentioned gift of a nail in deep gratitude for favors freely given and gladly received. The girls, like all Tahitians, were as fastidious as cats, but nonetheless found the hairy, gap-toothed, bad-smelling sailors sexually attractive, being fascinated by the contrast between the luminescent whiteness of their bared bodies and their mahogany-tanned faces and forearms. Getting the present of a nail was a bonus to an interesting experience.

The first man to escape the gunner's watchful eye, as Robertson remembered, was "a Dear Irish boy," one of the marines. A distinct drawback to Paddy's fun was that Tahitians felt no qualms about intimate intercourse in

70

public, so his sexual prowess was witnessed by a host of highly interested islanders, who passed comments in their native language. He got a thrashing from his shipmates for making such a rude exhibition of himself, but, as he confessed to the sailing master, he was too keen to attain "the Honour of having the first," to worry about a few spectators.

Those shipmates soon learned to disregard an audience, too. "The Women were far from being coy," remembered Midshipman Henry Ibbott — the young man who had lost his gold-laced hat — "For when a Man found a girl to his mind, which he might easily do Amongst so many, there was not much Ceremony on either side."

The agreed-on price was a four-inch nail, called "a thirty-penny nail," because four-inch nails cost thirty pence per hundred. Within a couple of weeks lusty seamen had prized so many four-inch spikes out of the hull that the ship was in danger of falling apart, and most were sleeping on the deck planks, as they had traded away their hammock nails, too.

This brisk trade in sex also meant that Fa'a had trouble finding provisions to trade with the gunner. Now that the islanders had another source of iron, they were much less eager to sell what they would normally be eating themselves, and, because no chief had formed an alliance with the Europeans, there was no one to order them to either go short or find some more. The price had gone up, too — because nails were now so abundant, their value had depreciated, and so the traders had set the price higher.

The same applied to the girls, who demanded bigger, longer nails for sex — a phallic symbol that eventually led to a lot of hilarity in the salons of London.

*Stage costume design for a Tahitian dancing girl,
de Loutherbourg*

# Chapter 7:
## "To give this royal isle its due"

On the first day of July, to complicate matters further, Fa'a vanished — "the Old Man was not at the Watering Place," wrote Wallis. For the *Dolphins*, this was an ominous development, as the "Old Man" was their only intermediary with the diminishing number of Tahitians who were still willing to sell the desperately needed provisions. Now that Fa'a had gone, the source of fresh food was under threat.

In fact, the old man had sailed to the district of Papara, in the south of the island, carrying a hatchet, some nails, and a coat, as evidence that he was still the middleman for the Europeans. His mission was to tell Amo and his advisor, the high priest Tupaia, everything that had happened since they had fled the scene of slaughter at Matavai Bay, along with the news that none of the northern nobles had managed to contact the paramount chief of the round-bottomed ship.

Obviously, it was an excellent chance for Amo to negotiate a treaty with the powerful strangers, thus preempting all the other chiefs who had been trying in vain to approach the high chief - *ari'i rahi* - of the strangers. Amo dismissed the idea, being very averse to another encounter with the men who had frightened him so much, but his wife, the chiefess, was much more receptive.

Purea, a statuesque, good-looking woman about thirty years old, whose full title was Te Vahine Airoro atua i Ahurai i Farepua, had a compelling personality, and a mind of her own. Noble Tahitian women were able to inherit property and rank, and Purea, who was an Ahurai princess with kin connections to the most powerful clans of Tahiti and Moorea, wielded power independently of her husband.

She also had very good political advice. About five years earlier, she had given birth to a son, and had gone against her husband's wishes by allowing the child to live, when it was customary for inconvenient babies to be smothered at birth. Amo had reluctantly consented to acknowledge the boy, named Teri'irere, but was so displeased with Purea that he turned away from her, and took a mistress.

And so she had taken a lover of her own - the priest Tupaia, who was a great diplomat and negotiator. Tupaia agreed with the old man that the chance to make an alliance with the powerful Europeans was one that should not be turned down, and so Fa'a returned to Matavai Bay, satisfied with the success of his mission.

*fine Pleasant weather the Old Man return to the Gunner and made signs to him that he had been up the Country to get the People to come in with Trade, soon after came down several people with larger Hogs than we had yet seen severall of which were sent Onboard the Old Man likewise came off and brought a roasted Hog with him as a present Gave him an Iron Pot looking glass, drinking Glass and several other things.*

— Captain Wallis, *Dolphin* journal, July 6, 1767

Tahitian Warrior Dugouts, from *Le Costume Ancien...*
Giulio Ferrario, 1827

Back in Papara, Tupaia and Purea were organizing a ceremonial voyage to Matavai Bay. Not only did they intend that the Europeans should be struck with awe and wonder, but it was necessary that the local chiefs were reminded of Purea's strength, wealth, and resourcefulness. On July 8, Robertson noted in his logbook, "This Day a Great Number of large Craft Come Round the SW point of the Bay, with Red & White and Blue Streamers flying."

The big double canoes were packed with people, and loaded heavily with provisions, and it was indeed a grand procession, as "ten or twelve" were double the size of the ceremonial canoe they had destroyed in the first attack. They were greeted in fine style too, a fleet of small craft coming out to greet them, while a host of people waited on the beach. "I am yet of a loss what to think of this fleet," the sailing master wrote as the regatta disappeared up a stream, unaware that he was witnessing the arrival of Purea, with Tupaia and the rest of her retinue.

He asked Captain Wallis whether he should take boats and follow the great canoes, but Wallis decided against the idea, for fear of confrontation and more loss of life. Probably for the same reason, Purea did the same, taking her time before accosting the strangers. Local dignitaries had to be recognized, and polite visits had to be paid to local chiefs, while she and her large retinue settled into the local *fare hau*, or conference hall, a magnificent pillared building set among the trees near the waterfront, which she had appropriated.

Then, having established herself, Purea took some chosen men to the river, and crossed it, imperiously waving the threatening muskets aside. Where the local nobility had failed Purea, Te Vahine Airoro atua i Ahurai i Farepua, was determined to succeed.

Once she had successfully invaded the European encampment, however, she was faced with the problem of which man to accost. Who was the *Dolphins'* leader?

Tahitians and Georgian Englishmen did have something in common — an acute recognition of nobility and rank. Both peoples placed great stock on what a person wore, as in both societies a man's clothing signified his status. In the Tahitians' case, this was the quality and color of the outer tapa robes, red being reserved for the highest chiefs. In the British navy, too, the nobility of the ship — the captain and his officers — habitually wore uniform, rather than dress like lower deck seamen. So, it was easy to tell the higher ranks from the commoners, because their dress was so much more magnificent - but which was the best uniform to approach? Which of these men was the greatest of them all?

Finally, Purea accosted the sergeant of marines, and presented him with ritual offerings of hogs, fowls, fruit, and tapa. It was a natural mistake, as Sergeant Gallagher's frock-coat was a splendid scarlet, the color sacred to 'Oro, the god of war, and the major deity in Tahiti at the time. Understandably, too, none of the Tahitian people had realized that the pale, pathetic figure who occasionally materialized at the stern windows of the ship was the captain of the *Dolphin*.

Sergeant Nicholas Gallager committed his own blunder, failing to recognize that the red color of Purea's outer *tiputa* — a long toga-like robe, made of one piece with a slit for the neck, and caught with a feathered sash at the waist — denoted nobility and authority in Tahiti. When she refused to accept any payment for the gifts, he simply sent them on board, without bothering to consider the implications.

It took a master's mate, John Gore, to realize that Purea was one of the Tahitian nobility.

John Gore, a 37-year-old American, was known for his quick temper, his sharpshooting, and his red hair. He was also very intelligent, a man who had passed his lieutenant's examinations in 1760, but still had not been commissioned. He had joined the first discovery voyage of the *Dolphin*, under Captain Byron, as a midshipman, had been promoted to master's mate within three days, and was now a valuable petty officer on the *Dolphin* under Captain Wallis.

Here, in Tahiti, he had been put in charge of the wooding party, with the job of collecting firewood, which involved more tact and diplomacy than might have been expected. The first time he had sallied out at the head of his gang, the islanders had become agitated, thinking he had come to cut down all their breadfruit trees, which was one of the traditional ways the victors in a tribal war wreaked their revenge. Gore placated the owner of the first tree with a seven-inch spike, and since then had devised a tactful method of "buying" the right to cut down a tree by tapping a spike into its trunk, and waiting to see if the owner would take it out. If he did, then the tree was "bought," and the woodsmen cut it down.

In the morning of Friday, July 10, Gore took his party to the northern side of the river, having spied a few likely old trees. As usual, he stuck a spike in one specimen, the elderly owner took it out, and the tree was cut down. Then came trouble, as the transaction had been closely watched by a number of chiefly spectators. According to the tale told to Robertson by one of the midshipmen, "another stout well lookt man who seemed to be one of their cheifs" strode up, and confiscated the nail from the old man.

The owner of the tree put up a vigorous protest, but rank prevailed; the chief refused to hand it back, and the old man went off to his house to sulk. Then Purea came out of the trees, accompanied by her lover and advisor, the high priest Tupaia. As Robertson recounted, "A few minutes after their came down a fine well lookt woman of the dark Mustee colour." The men who had watched the altercation told her the story, so she turned to the old man, "and she spoke to him a few words, but the old man scarce made any Answer, she then talkd to him that hade the nail, and immediately gave up the nail to the old man, and walkt of seeming in great fear and this Woman spok to him very Angery lyke, and soon after walkt in to the woods with the man who came down with her."

Having delivered justice, Purea calmly continued her stroll, and Gore and the other Europeans watched her go, feeling very impressed.

*Employed Wooding and otherwais as before, the Natives seemd very Displeased at our cutting their Breadfruit trees down but on giving a Nail for a Tree they were well satisfied and for a small Nail a Man carried it down to the Boats, got but very little trade, just enough for the Sick, two of the Inhabitants came of with the Wooders, one seemed to be a Chief, he dined with the Officers … This man we called Jonathan*

— Wallis, *Dolphin* logbook, July 9 (sea time), 1767

When the wooding party returned to the ship for their midday dinner, they brought two of the islanders with them. Robertson, who watched the visitors arrive, wrote that one "appeared to be a Chieff," because his companion, who was the lad they considered to be Fa'a's son, paid him so much respect. This "fine, well-made" chieftain, who was about thirty years old, "appeard to be a Sensable well behaved man."

He was certainly very intelligent, managing to express a great deal of curiosity about the ship. So Robertson and his friends gave him a tour, beginning from the railed poop at the stern, where it was partly shaded by the wooden awning, which also served as the quarterdeck, having a commanding view of the open deck below. Climbing down one of the two poop ladders, they walked past the capstan to the forecastle deck at the bow of the ship, where the anchors were stowed while the ship was at sea, and which was almost as high as the poop.

Robertson pointed out the great wooden masts and spars, trying to communicate the functions of the different parts of the impressive web of rope rigging, and then took them below decks, showing off the little cabins in the after part of the berth deck, where the officers and petty officers lived, then the amidships area where the marines slept, and finally the forward part where the common seamen kept their chests, slung their hammocks, and ate at swinging tables. They even clambered down into the hold, so Robertson could show off details of the hull, taking pleasure in the two Tahitians' open amazement at its solidness and vast capacity, so different from the shallow draft of their narrow canoes.

The party headed back up to the deck to dine in the gunroom, forward of the Great Cabin where the captain reigned, and also beneath the quarterdeck. Though there was no overhead skylight, sunlight streamed in through the gunports cut in the sides, so it was quite a pleasant, airy space, if cramped and cluttered and rather full of cannon.

Intrigued by the news of the Tahitian guests, both Captain Wallis and the first lieutenant, William Clarke, left their sickbeds to join them, and a good dinner was laid out. Then they set to, while the two young men were closely observed by most of the officers of the ship.

Before sitting down, the chief picked up the chair, and examined its construction from every angle. Then he put it down, sat on it, and gave the plates, knives, and forks the same scrutiny. According to Robertson, they were served a "very Excellent dinner, which consisted of Broth made with two fine fat fowls, two do. Rosted, a rosted pig, rosted yams, Plantains, Bananas Soft Bread, bisque apple pudding and apple pye — all of this he eate a part off, and took very great notice of the manner that we eate with our Spoons knives and forks, and used them in the same manner that we did and helpt him selfe with fowl pig yams etc the same as we did."

Considering that he had always used his fingers to eat, he coped very well, though Wallis observed that he did have a tendency to stick his fork in his ear. "We hade very

80

Good claret Madeira, port, Rum and Brandy Grog and excellent good London porter," Robertson went on, but though the islander tasted them all, he much preferred plain water, "and seemd greatly pleasd when we all toutched Glasses with him."

It was usual at the time for gentlemen to wipe their mouths with their pocket handkerchiefs before sipping from their glasses. Robertson reminisced with gusto that he noticed the chief was uncomfortable about this, having no handkerchief about his tapa garments, so solemnly handed him a corner of the tablecloth. The chief fell for the trick, and lifted it to wipe his lips.

This infuriated the first lieutenant, Mr. Clarke, who growled at the poor fellow for his gross behavior, shaking the cloth for emphasis. The Tahitian was embarrassed by his mistake, but still managed to display a robust sense of humor, making unambiguous signs that he would fetch a girl to sleep with the first lieutenant, to atone for his unintentional rudeness, and improve the officer's unpleasant mood.

According to Robertson, Clarke exclaimed, "Well done, Jonathan!" He was being sarcastic, because "Jonathan" was current English slang for an unsophisticated yokel, usually applied to an American colonial. However, it was a turning point in Anglo-Tahitian relations. As Robertson reminisced, for the first time a Christian name was bestowed on a native of the island. Others were not slow to follow. Master's mate Robert Molyneux recorded that the other guest, Fa'a's son, was given a name beloved by all sailors — "Jack."

The meal over, Wallis showed their chiefly visitor various coins, hoping to find that the Tahitians had a source of gold — "shewed him silver Gold & Brass but he knew nothing of it & preferred Iron before them all," he wrote with disappointment. Then they showed "Jonathan" a looking glass, and when he commenced to pull at his beard, the surgeon gave him a pair of tweezers, which he expertly put to use.

The most hilarious moment came when the doctor handed him a miniature of a pretty Englishwoman, joking that if he came to England with them, "he should have one of them always to Sleep with." This enraptured the young chief, who hugged and kissed the picture, while his hosts watched with condescending amusement.

Undoubtedly, he found their behavior equally odd. At sunset he was landed on shore, to be received by a huge, inquisitive crowd, and Robertson heard their roars of laughter as the young chief delivered a lively account of his adventure.

Jonathan was back at noon the next day, this time bringing *two* pretty girls, "which he brought off to Dinn with us." Welcoming the trio with gusto, Robertson and his friends gave them another tour of the ship, "and showed them everything that was curious supposing them to be his two Sisters, but when he came down to the Gun room he made us understand that he brought them off Agreeable to his promis, in order to make up maters with Mr Clark he offerd him the choice of eather."

Unfortunately, Robertson neglected to describe the first lieutenant's sniffish reaction, or the hidden laughter that this must have inspired. Next day, when Jonathan arrived on board alone, "we Enquired after the two young Girls and he made signs that they were crying Ashoar," evidently feeling dismissed and rejected. But, as he went on to communicate, "if the two Gentlemen who was most friendly to them would go ashore and sleep with them their, the young Girls would be very happy."

Again, Robertson neglected to say what happened after that, going on instead to describe fitting out Jonathan with a suit of European clothes. It was a job to get them onto his stalwart frame, "especially the Bretches," which puzzled him greatly, "but after he found out how to use them he seemd more fond of them than all the rest except the shoes." Once successfully shod, he walked up and down the deck, delighting in the noise he made, and after he was landed in one of the ship's boats, he made his friends carry him over the river, for fear of getting them wet.

That, unfortunately, was the last the Europeans saw of him — "what became of this Jolly young fellow afterwards we know not," wrote Robertson, "as we neaver saw nor heard anything more of him." The general supposition was that he had been forced to return to his home village, as otherwise he would be tempted to sail with the *Dolphin* when the ship left the island.

Which would have been a good thing, or so Robertson thought. "I dare say he would have soon learnd the England Language," he wrote, "and being a sensible fine smart man," he would have been able to tell them a lot more about his country than the *Dolphin*s could have learned on their own.

*Costume design for the character of Queen Oberea*
*— de Loutherbourg*

# Chapter 8:
## "My princess, or rather, my Queen"

*Fresh breezes and Rainy. Got only two Fowls, the Inhabitants all making signs for large Nails; in looking around the Ship the Carpenters found that all the belaying cleats were Ripped off & most of the Hammocoe nails drawn Ordered all hands up and endeavoured to find out who had been the /thieves, then told them if they would not discover it I would put a stop to their going onshore, could make no discovery*

— Captain Wallis, *Dolphin* journal, July 11, 1767

Because of the tales Jonathan told, and his shrewd deductions about what he had observed, the chiefess, Purea, and her confidante, Tupaia, understood the social situation on board the ship. To establish a political alliance, they had to pay a call on board, obviously. And finally, on Monday 13 July, Purea had her chance.

The gunner, William Harrison, had gone for a walk in the woods with one of the mates, Francis Wilkinson, as trade was so very slow that they were looking for farmers who would be willing to sell provisions. About two miles from the river they came across a prosperous village, where the houses were grouped about a great hall. Wilkinson, impressed, wrote, "It is ingeniously contrived & I believe has bin the Inhabitants of one of their Kings at

85

Present it is Inhabitants by A Woman whos Power seems to be equel to that of A Queen."

This was the *fare hau*, the district conference house Purea had commandeered. There, the two petty officers found Purea presiding over a grand feast, with what they guessed was as many as one thousand guests. Strangely, she was being fed by two women, seemingly unable to feed herself, but while they were still wondering about this, she broke off her repast to welcome them to join the banquet. When it was over she escorted Harrison and Wilkinson to the landing place, with her lover and advisor, Tupaia, and two other chiefs in attendance.

There, Purea arranged for two large hogs to be presented to the gunner. Then, that civility over, she firmly informed him that she wished to be taken on board the *Dolphin*.

Impressed by her regal bearing and the homage that had been paid to her by the locals during the elaborate feast, Harrison responded in a properly deferential manner. Ushering the noble quartet into a boat, he rowed them over, then gallantly assisted them up the ladder of battens nailed to the ship's side. After leading the way through the gunroom to the small corridor that formed the portico of the Great Cabin, he formally announced their presence to the marine who was standing sentinel at the captain's door.

Captain Wallis was at his desk, irritably estimating the number of nails that had been stolen from the ship, and writing up a reward for their recovery. Though sick and feeble and quite unprepared for royalty, he stood up politely when the gunner introduced "a tall well looking woman about fortyfive years old." Then, as he recognized Purea's "very majestic Mein," his overwhelming emotion was one of vast relief.

Samuel Wallis *needed* a Tahitian monarch, and up until this moment he had not been able to find one. With uneasy memories of the slaughter his cannon had inflicted, he knew his failure to establish a friendly détente with the islanders would lead to sharp criticism back in England. He could plead he had been forced to counter treachery with violence, but was aware that taking possession of the island "by right of Conquest" would not be considered good form. Since then, relations with the Tahitians had become chaotic, because of the exuberant consorting with the pretty girls, and the supply of provisions had become uncertain. What he needed was a native sovereign who would "cede" the country, then work with him to formalize the trading situation.

Like Robertson and everyone else on the ship, Wallis was under the misapprehension that the "king" had been killed when the ship's cannon had destroyed the ceremonial canoe that had led the first attack. Now, on the basis of no evidence whatsoever, apart from that "majestic Mein," he jumped to the conclusion that Purea was the dead king's "widow," a woman of the highest nobility, who by logic was the queen of all Tahiti.

He had no idea that he had drawn all the wrong conclusions. Not only was Purea's husband, Amo Tevahitua, alive and well, safely in seclusion in the district of Papara in the south of the island, but Tahiti did not have a reigning sovereign. No one was paramount ruler of the nation, though several district high chiefs, including Amo, Purea, and a local chief, Tutaha, had ambitions in that direction. The monarch Wallis needed did not exist.

Wallis searched his mind for an appropriate gift for this convenient queen — and was struck by divine inspiration. With unconscious cultural sensitivity, he sent for a length of cloth that he described later as "a large Blue Mantle that

Reached from her head to her Heels," and ceremoniously draped it around her shoulders.

He was phrasing it fancifully, as it was highly unlikely he carried any regal robes on board his overcrowded discovery ship (just in case he encountered a native monarch), and the "Mantle" was just a generous length of blue drilling, of the sort commonly stocked as trade goods, and used for making sailors' trousers. In his daily logbook, Samuel Wallis simply noted, "gave her some Cloth ribbons & other things, with wich she seem'd greatly pleased." But he could not have chosen better.

From Purea's point of view, the gesture was apt as well as flattering, because Wallis had recognized her power in a distinctively Polynesian way — at long last a European had satisfyingly complied with the Tahitian peacemaking ritual, by enfolding her with cloth. The gift also managed to be excitingly exotic, because the mantle was *blue*, a color only seen in rare butterflies, flowers, birds, and fish.

When Tahitians decorated their tapa just three plant-based dyes — red, yellow, and brown — were available to them, and of those red, being particularly difficult to manufacture, was reserved for *arioi* and nobility. Feathers were blue, and so were the sea, flowers, and sky, but never before the Europeans' arrival had the Tahitians seen the colors of sea and sky captured in cloth.

It is little wonder that Purea was "greatly pleased." More luckily still, she was a natural actress. An extremely intelligent woman - and advised by the perceptive Tupaia - she smoothly assumed the role of queen the *Dolphin*s had imagined for her, doing nothing to disturb a myth that existed only in their minds.

Tahiti might not have a supreme monarch, but she had the great satisfaction of playing the part, because who knew what it would lead to in the future? Obviously, cultivating this friendship was a priority, and pandering to the strangers' peculiar notions was no trouble at all. And not only did it guarantee a profitable friendship, but she could flaunt this special alliance simply by going on shore with the blue mantle about her shoulders.

Purea became not just the queen the Europeans needed, but their commercial agent, too, both Robertson and Wallis noting that a great many more foodstuffs were offered for sale, including dozens of hogs and hens, and an immense quantity of fruit.

"By their Assistance," wrote Francis Wilkinson, "we are not likely to Eat salt Meat while we are here."

"A representation of the surrender of the Island of Oteheite to Captain
Wallis by the supposed Queen Oberea," from Hawkesworth's *Voyages*

# Chapter 9:
## "The Queen's House"

*In the morning I went onshore for the first time where the Queen (I may call her) soon came, and made some of her people take me & all that went with me that were ailing in their Arms and carry me across the River, and so on to her house, I ordering a Guard to follow, there was a multitude of People, she only waving her hand, or speaking a word, they immediately withdrew and left us a free passage*

*When we came near her house a great number of Men and Women came out to meet her, and she brought them to me and after shewing me by signs they were her relations she took hold of my hand and made them kiss it.*

— *Dolphin,* Captain Wallis's journal, July 13, 1767

Captain Wallis did not really feel up to a formal state visit, but "the Queen" had so insistently invited him to visit her house that he agreed to go ashore. So, the next morning, he was rowed ashore with his officers, bearing a number of handsome gifts. Purea, who was waiting with her own entourage, instructed her attendants to carry the visitors over the river, a customary politeness Wallis imagined was a solicitous gesture because he and his officers were so obviously sick.

At the *fare hau* a great throng was waiting to greet them, providing a reassuring image for the British reading public — simply because it looked to the Europeans as if Purea had organized the "state visit" as a chance to formally cede the island to the conquerors. This was, of course, yet another fiction. In reality, the Europeans were simply welcomed and ushered into the *fare hau*, where both parties proceeded to thoroughly confuse each other.

Wallis and his officers, being practical seamen, measured the hall, making it 327 feet long, 42 feet broad, "and raised upon 39 pillars on each side, and 14 in the middle," and then he made a scale drawing of it, while the puzzled Tahitians politely watched. Purea summoned four girls, who coaxed the bemused captain and the sickest of his officers into shedding clothes and lying down, then delivered a healthful massage. So solicitous were they, the Englishmen were not allowed to dress themselves when this was over, the girls insisting on redressing them in their shirts, trousers, and coats, a process that was awkward for the men, and gave the girls a lot of trouble.

"She then ordered some Bundles to be brought, and took from them some Country Cloth, which is like paper," remembered Wallis. With her own hands Purea cut a *tiputa*, or Tahitian poncho, which she lifted over his head.

Wallis tried to stop her, not understanding the deep significance of enfolding him in tapa, but finally allowed her to swathe him in the toga-like garment, "not choosing to offend her." Then the acme of confusion was reached when the surgeon removed his wig to wipe his sweating head, striking the entire Tahitian assembly dumb with astonishment. As Wallis told the story after getting back to London, "the whole assembly stood for some time motionless, in silent astonishment, which could not have

92

been more strongly expressed if they had discovered that our friend's limbs had been screwed onto his trunk."

When it was time to go, Purea lifted Wallis in her arms, and carried him over wet and rough patches — "At my going away she ordered a very large Sow big with young to be taken down to the Boat. She accompany'd us & I choosing to walk, she took me by the Arm & lifted me over every Slough with as much ease as I could (when in health) a child," he wrote.

Despite a great deal of mutual bewilderment, and a complete inability to communicate, everything had gone very well indeed. Next morning Wallis sent a present of "Six Hatchetts Six Billhooks and some other things," on shore with the gunner, and in return Purea's chief minister, Tupaia, arranged for provisions to be delivered to the trading tent.

The gunner was forced to pay more than usual for the hogs and chickens, but that was not Purea's fault, as Wallis admitted—it was the ship's "people spoiling the Market."

But, even with inflation taken into account, everything was still "as cheap as dirt."

The Europeans, meantime, had gained some idea of both the name of the "queen" and the name of the island. As Tahitians used the syllable "O" to mean "this is," both were preceded by that letter, so that Tahiti was "Otaheite" and Purea was "Oberea," but everyone was happy, as it was a sign of friendly familiarity.

Of more consequence, Purea disappeared from sight, along with her advisor and the rest of her attendants. Some alarm was felt, as the supply of provisions promptly dried up. Wallis sent out Furneaux with party of sixty armed men to scout the perimeters of the bay in an almost fruitless quest for alternative sources of provisions, but on

July 18 he was able to note with distinct relief that Purea and her retinue had reappeared. Evidently they had been "upcountry" to organize more trade, because the copious supply of provisions resumed.

> *Moderate & fair. Employed as before, got fourteen Small Hogs a Dozen of Fowles & as many Bananas Plantains Apples and Breadfruit as will last for two Days for eating and boiling. Served fresh Pork — this day the Queen shewed herself again she having been absent some days — and soon after a number of People came with trade — the Gunner sent off fourteen Hogs & plenty of fruit.*

> — Captain Wallis, journal, *Dolphin*, July 18, 1767

On the same day that Purea reappeared on the beach, Sergeant Gallagher and one of the midshipmen, Richard Pickersgill, took a stroll to the *fare hau*, where they found Purea presiding over another vast feast.

"Mr Pickersgill tould me the Dinner was drest at some distance where there was several little Houses," wrote Robertson. "When it was ready they all formd a Ring and set doun round the Queen, who was sited on a very fine matt with two very handsom Young Ladys standing by her."

When the food was served, Purea first ordered the two young attendants to give it to men who were evidently acting as waiters, for they handed it around the great throng, beginning first with those who sat next to "the Queen," and then to those who seemed to be of a slightly lesser rank, and so on down to the commoners, "and the Whole Eat very hearty." These who were dining first were all men.

94

Finally, food was placed directly before Purea, "who invitd Mr Pickersgill and the Serjent to Eate with her, but they Excused themselves and pointed to some fresh fruit which was Just puld off the trees."

Shrugging away this impoliteness, Purea told her two young attendants to feed her, "which they did, the one stood at the Right Hand and the oyther at the left, and fed her by turns with their hands only." The one who stood at the right would wash her hand in a basin of clean water, then pick up a piece of meat, "and put it in Queens mouth," and then wash her hand again. And throughout this arduous process, "she Eate very hearty, but touchd no meat with her own hands."

Obviously, this strange custom was some local ritual. Once the queen had finished, the two young attendants settled down to eat their own meals, and when they were done the women of the multitude were at last allowed to satisfy their appetites. "And after that the servants set doun and dinned at a great distance." The whole affair was conducted in an unearthly silence, but once everyone had eaten his or her fill, and the mess was cleared away, the air was filled with happy chatter.

Having witnessed this very foreign ceremonial feast, and observed how obsequiously Purea was treated, there was no way Pickersgill and Gallagher would have refused when she conveyed a wish that she go on board the *Dolphin* again. As thoroughly intimidated as the gunner earlier, the sergeant of marines and the midshipman were glad to comply.

This time, Wallis was confined to his berth, far too ill to receive visitors, so it was Robertson who received them at the gangway, and it was he, with Pickersgill, who entertained the royal party in the gunroom.

"She brought a very good present of live stock Onbd, which Served all hands two days," he wrote. Captain Wallis, hearing about it, ordered that a good present of something made of iron be given to her in return.

Purea declined the offer of food, possibly because she was inhibited by Tahitian common law, which prohibited women from eating with men, or perhaps because she was under a temporary taboo where she had to be fed by female attendants, not being allowed to touch her own head. Her companions, though they had eaten well at the feast, did hearty justice to the meal. Like Jonathan, they rejected rum and brandy, preferring water, but appeared to like Madeira wine, of which they drank two glasses each.

They managed to express some curiosity about how the food was roasted, because after the dinner was cleared away Robertson took the Tahitians to the galley, which was at the foot of the foremast, under the shelter of the forecastle deck. A wonderful aroma wafted out to greet them, because a pig and two hens were being roasted in this ship's kitchen — "they all vewed very Attentively," he wrote, "and Laughd very hearty, one of the Men laid hold of the Spit and turned it round three times."

Naturally, the Tahitians, who were used to leaf-wrapped meat steamed in an earth oven, were most intrigued. While their companion was trying his hand at turning the spit, the others examined the two immense copper cauldrons, which fortunately had been cleaned to a brilliant shine. Then, after foiling an attempt to pry off a piece of the copper, Robertson and the midshipman ushered the party along the weather deck and up the ladder to the quarterdeck, to show them the ship's fowls in their coops.

Features of the rigging were then pointed out, "which," as Robertson remembered later, "Surprized them the most of anything. In my oppinion the whole was Smart Sensable people and very cureous in observing everything which they saw, but the Queen was rather more so nor any of the rest," he continued, going on to describe Purea in detail, as "a strong well made Woman about five foot ten Inches high, and very plainly dressed, without eather Shoes Stockings or head dress, and now kind of Jewels or trinkets about her."

Somehow, the large, handsome and persuasive master managed to inspect her entire outfit — "her undergarments was white which I shall call her Skirt, her petecoat was White and Yellow, and her Gown was Red, which was the Mournings, which she wore for her Husband, who was killd in the Great double Canoe which gave the Signal for the Attack when they thought to have taken our Ship from us."

Despite jumping to this strange conclusion that the color of nobility was mourning dress, the sailing master expressed no surprise that the supposed widow "appeard very cheerful and merry all the time she was Onboard."

When sunset arrived, and it was time for the party to leave, Captain Wallis sent orders that the Queen and her retinue should be taken on shore in the ship's barge. As he was feeling a little better, he decided to accompany them, and Purea seized the chance to further demonstrate to the locals that the *ari'i rahi* of the ship was her particular friend. As Captain Wallis noted in his logbook, "she harrangued the People taking me & the Officers in her arms & shaking us by the hand & pointing to the ship."

Robertson testified that "not a Whisper" could be heard as she spoke. "When she ended her Speech she pointed to the Capt and all the Officers who was along with him, and made her people understand that they were the principle people belonging to the Ship. She then took her Leave with a short speech and marchd off with a great number of the people Attending her.

"Both the Queen and all her Attendance Went off Extreemly well pleasd with the reception they got onbd the ship, as a Confirmation of this, we got more Stock this afternoon nor any three days before, in all we got forty Eight Hogs and pigs, four dozen of fowls and a great Quantity of all sorts of fruit."

# Chapter 10:
# "But hark! The Boatswain's call so shrill"

> When I was Ordering the liberty men into the boat
> the Carpenter came and tould me every cleat in the Ship
> was drawen, and all the Nails carried off. At same time
> the Boatswain informed me that the most of the
> hammock nails was drawen and two thirds of the men
> oblidged to lie on the Deck for want of nails to hang their
> Hammocks
>
> — Robertson, journal, *Dolphin*, July 21, 1767

Two days later, again according to George Robertson's reminiscences, Purea and "one of her principal attendants" - Tupaia, the high priest - paid another visit to the *Dolphin*. They arrived very early, at eight in the morning, and were immediately ushered into the Great Cabin, where Captain Wallis ordered a breakfast set. When the food arrived, Tupaia stood up to say prayers. He made a long speech, gesturing about the cabin, and then went into the quarter gallery and looked out the windows and spoke to the sun.

His prayers and oration ended with a ritual offering to the gods — sitting down at the table, the priest plucked up some butter in his long nails, and cast it down in the traditional manner. Lieutenant Clarke furiously snatched the dish of butter away, and ordered the captain's servant to bring a fresh one, an insult so offensive that Tupaia sat stiff and silent, refusing to touch any more food.

To mollify Purea, who was also greatly affronted, Robertson took her on a tour of the accommodations, making her a present of anything that took her eye, including a fancy ruffled shirt. He helped her put this on, pulling it over her head and showing her how to put her arms through the sleeves, a novelty that – or so he reckoned - "gaind her heart."

When he delivered her back to the Great Cabin, as he further reminisced, she approached Wallis, "looking upon him as our King," and requested him to "Signe a Treaty of Peace in order to settle all Differences betwixt her Maj$^s$ people and ours" — something that could not possibly be true, as Tahitians had no concept of writing, let alone the legal value of a signature. Robertson explained away the lack of a signed treaty by claiming Wallis had a paralytic disorder of his writing hand, but no such document ever existed.

More convincing is the master's memory that Purea decided to check his stalwart frame for tattoos. Good-naturedly, Robertson bared his legs and arms, and then his chest, which she was amazed to find was furry. Impressed by his size and strength, she called to Tupaia to come and feel his muscles, "which I allowed him to do, and he seemd greatly Astonished as well as She."

The two Tahitians discussed it for a while, and then Purea turned to Robertson, put her arms around him, and tried to lift him up. He foiled her by making himself a dead weight, so her advisor "made a Sign for me to Lift her," which Robertson did, effortlessly carrying her round the cabin, much to her delight. As he smugly went on to theorize, "this is the way the Ladys here trys the men, before they Admit them to be their Lovers."

Then she made signs that she wanted to go back on shore. As Wallis was not well, Robertson was ordered to take the barge and escort Purea and her companion to her house, "but not to stay any time, as he and both the Lieut<sup>s</sup> was in a bade state of health." There was the usual throng of natives waiting at the landing place, and Purea introduced Robertson to the local dignitaries, instructing them to shake hands with him: "We then set out Arm in Arm for the Palace, and all the Principale part of the Inhabitance came after us."

At the *fare hau* the procession was received by yet another crowd. Speeches were made, "and all the people formd a Ring round us and Seemd highly pleasd." Food was cooked for a fine feast and Purea took Robertson in one hand and Pickersgill with the other and led them to a fine mat, where they all sat down. "She then made Another Speech and a great number of the principale people Stood round, and gave great Attention to what she said."

Then there was an even more unusual development. An elderly noblewoman was enticed to feel Robertson's muscular legs and thighs, and run her long fingernails through his chest hair ,which caused her to cry out, "Oh. Oh." Robertson and the old lady then shook hands, and Robertson received a flirtatious invitation to tarry, one that he had no trouble turning down.

Getting up, he walked over to the "queen's palace," and, seamanlike, set to measuring it, "and found it be a House of three hundred and twenty one foot Long, and thirty six foot Broad neatly built and supported with fourteen large pillers of Wood, in the middle of the House. Every pillar was about fifteen or sixteen Inches diameter and about twenty four foot high." And not only that, but they were "very neatly carved."

This was followed by a rather tense episode, in which a young noble demanded to inspect Robertson's sword, which he gave over very reluctantly, taking "care to keep one of the pistols cockt ready in my hand." The young chief tried out the edge, flourished it about his head a few times, and then was so reluctant to give it back that Robertson had to wrest it out of his grip, which "made him a look a little surly."

A demonstration of whirling round and slicing the top off a plantain did the trick, as the young chief took fright and made a rapid departure. This was followed by a suspenseful pause, as Robertson aggressively looked around with the sword in his hand, but all was saved by Purea, who "Laughed very hearty," reassuring the crowd, who "smiled and seemd pleased."

After another inspection of the "Palace," where a lot of mundane activities, such as pulping breadfruit, were taking place, Robertson decided it was time to go, and approached the "Queen" to say farewell. As amiable as ever, Purea claimed him by cutting a *tiputa*, throwing it over Robertson's head, and tying it with a sash. Then, having made a short speech in which she pronounced him as a friend, she presented him with sixteen yards of tapa.

Remembering the captain's instructions, Robertson turned down the elderly noblewoman's invitation to stop and dine. The unintentional discourtesy took the old woman so greatly aback that she made "very plain Signs" that Purea would be his bed companion that night, if only he would stay.

Both women smiled understandingly when the master declined, but his appearance of gentlemanly virtue was quite ruined when he stopped to flirt with a particularly fair maiden on the path to the beach. Purea, obviously miffed, drew him away, and firmly saw him into his boat.

When Robertson returned to the ship, it was to find that the traders had brought twelve hogs on board, along with some fowls and an abundance of fruit. Unusually, he ordered that the fowls and some of the fruit were to be given to the men, but the hogs and the rest of the fruit were to be "put by to Carry to Sea." While the socializing with the Tahitians and the trading for goods had been going on, the ship had been cleaned and overhauled. And now, for several good reasons, it was time to leave Tahiti.

> *Pinckney Seaman two Nights ago Drew of with a Crow the Belaying Cleat of the Main Sheet under the Half Deck, and on their detecting him he begged them not to tell & he would Nail it up again, however was gone in the Morning — this he could not deny, but said he immediately Nailed it in its place, and that someone else must have stole it & that as for the other Cleats that were ripped off he knew nothing of — however as he was detected in drawing it off and on searching his Chest found a great Number of the Country fish Hooks, and a Collection of large Shell which the Inhabitants don't part with without Nails or Iron — which am certain he could not come at honestly therefore by way of Example, made him run the Gantlett three times round the Deck — as a proper reward for his crime — Served fresh Pork & fruit.*
>
> — Wallis, logbook on the *Dolphin*, July 21, 1767

That night, Robertson, standing on the forecastle deck above the galley, had overheard some men who were waiting to collect their suppers accuse six other sailors of spoiling the trade in sex by giving bigger nails to the girls. The sextet spiritedly defended themselves by claiming they got double value for double-sized spikes, and the argument turned into a brawl. Robertson jumped down and broke up the fight, but after consultation with the officers it was decided that one of the six — a hapless fellow by the name of Francis Pinkney, found guilty prying off a wooden belaying cleat to steal the nails that secured it — should serve as an example for the rest, by running the gauntlet three times around the ship.

At noon Robertson ordered the men into a double line, armed with nettles (light ropes used in sailmaking), and Francis Pinkney was launched into a dash between the two rows, while the men flailed feebly at his back. The reason for their "merciful" play with the nettles was that Pinkney had staunchly refused to implicate any of the others, or so the master deduced. Robertson gave him a thump that jerked a few names out of him, and led to a much harder drubbing on the next run of the gauntlet.

*This day the Queen came Onboard again, & insisted on going to her House, she brought with her severall Hogs & would take nothing in return — I Shured I would go onshoar in the Morning, which I did with severall Officers, & was carried up to her House. I brought a hansome present of Hatchetts BillHooks knives buttons threds needles scissars — a Shirt a Piece of Broad Cloth and many other things — she made me the Two Liuts & Purser who had been all ill sit down & called a Number of her attendants & they Chafed our Legs thighs sides & Necks for near half an Hour, after which she tied Presents of hair round our Hatts, & a Bunch of Cocks feathers which I saw none wear but herself, & sent after us a Large Hog & a Sow Big with Pig — fruit of all sorts*

— Wallis, logbook on the *Dolphin*, July 22, 1767

Any sane and sensible captain would have agreed with George Robertson that it was high time the ship finished provisioning and sailed away from this over-amorous isle. When Purea came on board with her imperious invitation to make a ceremonious visit to the *fare hau*, however, Wallis summoned his best manners, and agreed to pay a call in the morning.

Wallis's logbook description is at first a curious echo of the formal visit of 13 July, as described in his journal eight days before. Again, he arrived on the riverbank with a retinue of officers, carrying his "hansome present." Again, Purea had them carried over the river, and again "she made me the Two Lieut[s] & Purser who had been all ill sit down & called a Number of her attendants & they Chafed our Legs thighs sides & Necks for near half an Hour."

What followed was new, however, and very much more solemn. Signing to her guests to be seated, Purea removed their cocked hats, and attached tufts of sacred feathers to them. Then she wreathed their bared heads with twisted cords made of plaited human hair — a powerfully symbolic gesture, as she made signs "it was her hair & her own work."

The head of any person was considered sacred - *tapu* - as it was the seat of their psychic force - *mana*. But, because of a chief's close connection with the gods, anything to do with his or her head was encompassed by some of the most terrifying taboos of Polynesian society. Cutting a chief's hair was so fraught with danger, the barber's hands could not be used for anything else for a certain prescribed time.

Indeed, that she had been using her own hair to make these cords could be the reason Purea could not feed herself, and had to be fed by others. But her intentions were serious. Now, as advised by her lover, the high priest

Tupaia, she was playing out her own intensely significant act of possession, using her sacred hair to bind and capture the powerful Europeans.

Still more of great psychological significance was to come. After they had all arrived back at the landing place, Purea beckoned to some servants, who stepped forward bearing "a Large Hog & a Sow Big with Pig," both signs of a fertile union. She had already given the men the fine, intricately patterned mats they had been seated on, a gift as symbolic as the presentation of tapa. These were loaded into the boat, and to all appearances the visit was over.

Then Wallis completely spoiled the occasion, by signing that he would sail away in four days' time. Horrified, Purea urged him to delay long enough for a visit to Papara. As Wallis noted in his log, she "pointed to the Country, & shewed she was going there & made signs for us to stay Twenty or 15 days but on my shewing her that four days was the time she sat down & cryed very much."

The tears were sincere. Advised by Tupaia, Purea had invested a great deal of thought, wealth, and prestige into establishing an *entente* with the Europeans. It was critical for her local standing that Wallis should make a formal "state" visit to her own territory, but Captain Wallis, who had no idea that she was a co-ruler only, and of another district entirely, was adamant in his refusal.

It was time to take his sexually sated and increasingly combative men away, and he obstinately shook his head, despite her increasingly desperate pleas.

The weather turned squally and rainy, but preparations for departure went ahead. Anchors were weighed, until the *Dolphin* was held by only her best bower, and the topgallant masts and yards — the most lofty parts of the rigging, which had been struck (unrigged) and stored while the ship was at anchor — were sent up again. Hogs, pigs, and poultry were brought on board in such abundance that the decks of the ship looked, sounded, and smelled like a barnyard. Great bunches of bananas were strung in the rigging, while the holds were packed with hay the men had cut and dried for the animals, and with plantains and breadfruit.

> *the Gunner sent of no less than Twenty Hogs with great Plenty of fruit, Our Decks quite full of Hogs and fowles, kill the small & keep the large for sea, they nor the fowles will eat nothing but fruit, the Gunner desired a present for the Old man who hath been very usefull to him, gave him an Iron Pott some Hatchetts & Bills and a piece of Cloth, the Gunner hopes that the Old Man will let his son go with us as he seems inclined so to do & the Boy very willing.*
>
> — Wallis, logbook on the *Dolphin*, July 22, 1767

On July 25, while all this was going on, Wallis very belatedly remembered orders given to him by their Lordships of the Admiralty to "obtain a complete knowledge of the Land or Islands supposed to be situated in the Southern Hemisphere." This meant listing plants, animals, and people, and charting the territory, with particular attention paid to anything that might reap riches for England in the future, such as export-worthy crops, pearls, and metal ores.

He summoned John Gore, and sent him off with a party of forty seamen and Fa'a as a guide, to penetrate as much of the hinterland as he could reach before nightfall, and then to return the next day. Robertson, who was busy with another project at the time, reminisced later, "This was the

107

first and Last Attempts that we ever made to discover the Inland Country."

Robertson's project was a precursor of what lay in the future for Europeans in Tahiti. The purser, John Harrison (no relation of the gunner), a remarkable man of astronomical bent, had worked out a surprisingly accurate position of the island, finding its longitude by "taking the Distance of the Sun from the Moon and working it according to Dr. Masculine's method which we did not understand" — as Captain Wallis, like everyone else in the ship, frankly admitted.

Harrison was able to do it because he had a pre-publication copy of an ephemeris compiled by the Astronomer Royal, Dr. Nevil Maskelyne, this being an almanac listing the daily positions of the heavenly bodies. The previous evening, while leafing curiously through this book, Robertson had noticed there was an eclipse of the sun due next day, and had applied to Captain Wallis for permission to go on shore and take observations. This was readily given, so at daybreak Robertson and Harrison set out with a telescope fitted with a dark glass, and Midshipman Pinnock to assist.

Just as they had ended their observations and made their calculations, Purea and "one of her chiefs" - evidently Tupaia - arrived to see what they were doing. Robertson offered them the telescope, and they both looked at the sun. The master enjoyed their open amazement, so after removing the dark glass he refocused the instrument on various parts of the bay, and handed it over so the two Tahitians could marvel at the enlarged views.

Then Tupaia wanted another look at the sun. Allowing his rough sense of humor to get the better of kindness or good sense, Robertson deliberately neglected to put back the dark glass before aiming the telescope at the full sun and beckoning Tupaia to have a look, "which almost blinded the poor man."

To confuse him still further, Robertson studied the sun himself (after surreptitiously replacing the glass), "then Looked him full in the face as if I hade been Surprized at his not being able to look."

> *Squally with rain, the latter fair — Sent the Queen two Turkeys, Two Geese, three Guinea Hens, a Cat big with Kitten, some China, Glass bottles, Shirts, Needles, thread, Cloth ribbons Pease Calivances and about sixteen sorts of Garden seeds as cabbages, turnips etc. The Guner took up two Marines with Shovels and made a large Bed and planted a little of all sort in it and gave her the Queen the seeds and a Shovel several of the Garden Seeds and pease we knew would grow as he planted some in many places that were very flourishing I likewise sent her two Iron Potts, knives, scissors and Spoon*
>
> — Wallis, journal on the *Dolphin,* July 24, 1767

The following afternoon Gore and his party had still not returned, so Purea and her attendants were invited on board the *Dolphin*. Wallis frankly admitted his ulterior motive for this, writing in his journal, "I thought by securing her and some of the Principal People there would be no danger to the Party." In effect, Purea, Tupaia, and a number of other chiefs were being kept hostage against Gore's safe return.

There was another even darker reason — suspicions had been expressed in the gunroom that the reason Purea was so anxious for them to stay was that she planned to attack and seize the ship.

George Robertson was furious, expostulating, "what reason my Shipmates has for this unCharitable Conjecture I know not, But this fact I am Certain, since our first Aquantance with this Great Woman, we have got three times the quantity of Refreshments that we did Before and the whole of the Natives is now friendly & Sociable" — but Wallis and his officers did not agree with him.

> *After the Observation was taken went to the Queen's house and shew'd her the Telescope, she looked thro' it & was all astonishment then made many of her attendants look thro' it — after this I invited her & many of her Court to come onboard which they accepted, I thought by securing her and some of the Principal People there would be no danger to the Party that I sent off Entertain'd them with a good Dinner, she eat nothing nor would she drink, all the others eat very hearty, but drank only water.*
>
> — Wallis, journal on the *Dolphin*, July 25, 1767

Another reason for caution was that the natives were restless. Francis Wilkinson had been the first to note, "The Indians suspecting that we Ware going Away" were assembling in multitudes on the beach and the over-looking hills, and becoming agitated at the prospect of losing this source of so much gossip and iron.

According to Wilkinson's shipmate, George Pinnock, the gunner "sent word off that ye natives began to grow very Numerous, verry obstinate & troublesome." Captain Wallis promptly ordered him to take down the trading tent and come on board with his party.

No sooner had the gunner arrived, than he was given yet another order, to load and ready the cannon in the waist of the ship, just in case force was needed. It was then, as an added precaution, that Wallis invited Purea and her attendant chiefs on board, on the pretext of a farewell dinner.

Purea scarcely noticed the atmosphere of distrust. While the chiefs with her "eat very hearty" (though without taking wine or grog), she was doing her utmost to prevail on Wallis to stay just ten days longer. Again and again he refused, and every time she wept bitterly. Undoubtedly, he was relieved when, at about five in the evening, Gore and his party materialized on the beach, as it enabled him to pry Purea away from the arms chest, where she crouched wailing loudly.

It was not even as if Gore's excursion had been worth all the fuss and bother. He had brought back a small quantity of ginger and turmeric and a few black rocks that just might hold some sort of mineral, but otherwise had little to report, except that the accessible land up the river was heavily inhabited and closely cultivated, and it was very hard going after they got into the foothills of the mountains.

So Wallis sent Purea and her party on shore.

> *In the evening when our People had returned from the Excursion they had made into the Country & come down to the Beach, I took the Queen & her attendants & put them into the Boat and sent them onshore.*
>
> *The Queen expressed great sorrow when she found that we persisted in leaving this place, and made Signs that she would be here again tomorrow morning*
>
> — Wallis, journal on the *Dolphin*, July 25, 1767

111

Purea and Tupaia did not go far at all. Next morning, as Robertson noted in his logbook, John Gore "found the old Lady on the Beach." She and her attendants had slept there—for fear, Robertson said, "of not seeing us before we Sail'd."

Accordingly, she was able to do one last service for the ship. Francis Wilkinson was sent in charge of a boat's crew to fill the last few barrels with water, but was fearful of landing, because the beach was so packed with people. Purea saw his predicament, and with an imperious wave sent the mob to the far side of the river.

Then, when Wilkinson was about to pull off again, she tried to bribe him with some large hogs to carry her to the ship in his boat, but his instructions were not to take any islanders on board, so he steadily refused.

> She presently Launched a Double Canoe and came of to the Ship, on which about fourteen or sixteen more were launched and followed when she came off she cried a great deal, she came in and Staid about an hour, there Springing up a breeze weighed the Anchor, and made Sail we then sent her into her Boat, She greived extreamly at it, embraced us all in the most affectionate Manner, as did all her attendants who seemed to be very sorrowfull at our leaving them, soon after it fell calm, sent the Boats a Head, the Canoes returned to the Ship again and the One which the Queen was in made fast to the Gunroom Port, and she came into the Bow of it where she sat crying we gave her many usefull things, which she Accepted, yet made little account of them being under so much affliction

> — Wallis, journal on the *Dolphin*, July 27, 1767

Undeterred, Purea, with Tupaia and several others from her retinue, boarded a large canoe, which was paddled across the lagoon toward the ship. They were in good time to hear the shouting as the men were mustered to the capstan, then rhythmic chanting as brawny fists shoved on the capstan bars. By sheer muscle-power the ship was eased up to the straightening anchor chain, until the bower was a-peak, on the verge of leaving the bottom.

More shouts, and more seamen, fit and muscular from five weeks in Tahiti, scrambled up the rigging, and side-stepped along the yards to loosen the sails. A loud rattle as the great sheets of canvas dropped, and squeals as the yards were braced around. Slowly, the ship began to move forward, plucking the rest of her anchor chain as she came, and up the anchor surged, in a sudden scent of seaweed and saltwater, dripping black Tahitian sand as it clattered against the side of the ship.

The wind was very light, forcing the *Dolphin*s to lower three boats, and tow the ship through the gap in the reef. Then at last the sea breeze gusted. The boats were hoisted aboard and stacked one inside another on top of the skids, amidships, and the yards were squared for the open sea.

Jibs rippled and snapped, great square sails billowed and tautened. An incoming swell lifted and dropped her hull in a farewell curtsey, and the *Dolphin* was on her way.

# Chapter 11:
## "Up anchors, boys, your topsails fill"

*at Ten a breeze sprung up & we took leave of the Queen, & all our worthy friends — there were thousands on the Hills looking after us — at Noon Port Royal Bore SE by E 4 Leagues—*

— *Dolphin,* Captain Wallis's logbook, July 27, 1767

While the departure from Tahiti had gone smoothly, there was dissension on the quarterdeck of the *Dolphin*.

Back on June 19, when the ship had been approaching Tahiti, some of the men had imagined they could see mountains in the south, about sixty miles away. It would have been nothing but a cloud formation, this being a common phenomenon in the Pacific, but these men — including the master, Robertson — were convinced that it meant that Tahiti was a peninsula of the great south land. Accordingly, Robertson and the other officers argued for a southward course.

As their Lordships of the Admiralty were to learn to their displeasure, however, Samuel Wallis lacked the soul of a discoverer. As his officers knew very well, his explicit instructions were to explore "the Southern Hemisphere between Cape Horn and New Zealand," in an effort to discover the fabled *Terra Australis Incognita*, which would have brought them all fame and fortune.

115

But he chose to disregard them. It should have been possible to find the islands of New Zealand, as they were already partially laid down on a map. But even though he had a gifted amateur astronomer on board, in the shape of his purser, he decided not to face the challenge of locating them, then making many lunar observations, and drawing up an accurate chart.

He was probably well aware by then that Tahiti was an island. Not only was he an experienced seafarer, with an instinct for the movement of currents and winds that betrayed the presence of land over the horizon, but Purea's advisor, Tupaia, who had picked up English very quickly, and was also a well-travelled star navigator, would have made it clear.

There were other excuses, including his own bad health. Careening the *Dolphin* in Matavai Bay had found her copper-sheathed bottom as clean as the day she had left the shipyard, but she was leaking a lot more than on the way out. "Found that the Ship makes much much more water than she did before we put into Port Royal," he wrote on July 29, 1767; and again, on 3 August, "in fine weather we pump Every watch, but when it blows fresh every two Hours or Oftener … the water coms so clear up that we wash the decks with it." This was entirely due to the shaky state of her hull. Because so many nails had been pried out of the ship, the planks worked in and out with the motion of the waves.

He could not plead lack of provisions, however. Because of Purea's patronage and Tupaia's organization, the *Dolphin* was lavishly stocked with fresh food and fresh water; and as a result of five weeks of eating well, all his men were scurvy-free.

The truth of the matter was that, like his predecessor, John Byron, he lacked the true discoverer's zeal to drive his ship and his men into unimaginable dangers.

Meantime, he set to writing the first draft of "A more particular Account of the Inhabitants of Otaheite, and of their domestic Life, Manners, and Arts," something, as he was uneasily aware, would be demanded by the Admiralty when he got home. He had to consult with his officers, as he readily admitted, having been confined to his berth so much of the time they had been there, but they were happy to oblige.

**"Remarks made at King George the 3<sup>d</sup> Island in Latitude of 17:30 S and Longitude from London of 152:00'W, by Observation at Port Royal,"** he began.

"The whole time we have been at this Island the Master or Mates have whenever a Boat could be spared been landing & making remarks. Lieut. Furneaux with a Guard of as many Men as could be spared hath been alongshore three or four Leagues both to the Eastward & Westward of the Ship, untill he was taken ill and then Mr Gore the Mate was sent to look into the Rivers & falls of water, the Plains, Mountains Valleys and Woods directly back, their Reports to me were as follows —

"Lieut Furneaux sais that all the way alongshore and in many Places a Mile or a Mile & half back that the country is exactly the same as it is here at the Landing Place — that between every Mountain runs a river or rivulet but none Navigable, the Plain is full of Breadfruit CocoaNutt, Plantain & apple trees, other shrubs very coarse, which they make no use of their Houses neat and plantations of Trees for Cloth neatly fenced of as it is here, the Country

117

full of inhabitants, they had Hogs & Cocks in Plenty but he saw neither Hens Chicken or Eggs (nor did any of our people that have been in the Mountains, yet we have had both hens & Chickens brought onboard (but not one Egg)

"he saw no other animal except Dogs & Ratts the latter of which are innumerata but they don't trouble themselves about them, the Grass seemed to be very good & is great plenty.

"Fish were small Mullet, Crawfish of two Pound, abundance of Shell fish and some Parret fish and others we have no name for, but all kinds of fish are scarce here for tho' we tried with Seines Trall, Line and every other Method I don't remember any but One Shark that was caught all the time we lay here.

"Mr Furneaux sais that they had abundance of Boats Built & building many sixty feet Long, that the people were very civil & no way molested them except their Numbers which Novelty had made follow him, that they gave the Cocoa Nutts breadfruit ready drest & Roasted Hogs, that as there was a market established at our watering place the Natives seemd rather inclined to carry their Hogs & Poultry there than sell them at their own houses, in his way back he went up the sides of severall Hills & found what was cultivated was very fertile, the Soil appearing to be fine rich reddish & Brownish Earth, that they had very large well tasted yams, but he saw None Growing, the people made the Signal that they were not in Season

"some of the seamen told him they saw some large Pearls in the Ears of the Natives, but he could not find them, he got Six Small ones but sadly Mangled in boreing Holes thro' them, this was all his report, excepts that, he saw ducks, Herons, Parretts & Green Doves & some small Birds, their Burying Places were walled in with Stone and

118

had at one End tall Trunks of Trees with Ten or a Dozen Men badly carved on them one over the other, the same we find near the ship,

"he sais that the Plantations further to the Westward appear to be better cultivated than those nearer the ship as the country is leveler & goes back with an easy ascent some Miles whereas it is More Mountainous here; besides the Reefs that run of here affords subsistence for Multitudes of inhabitants, for they go out on the Reef with a little bread at low water and catch small fish, & shell fish which they Break and eat immediately, & so much time is lost every day which would otherwise be Employed in cultivateing the Ground.

"They have no kind of Metal amongst them, their Knives are Mussell Shells which they cut up their Meat with, fixe their Apples Breadfruit &c & kill Hogs & Fowles with, for axes and adzes they grind Stones into the Shape of an Adze, & work extreamley well with them, the build Canoes very Neat, & sew the Planks together with Cocoa Bark & make holes with Bone ground sharp."

This topic of the Tahitians' boats, being much closer to Wallis's seafarer's heart, was tackled with more interest and alacrity.

"Their Mast Steps in the Middle & the Sail is made of a Mat, the Riggin of Cocoanut Bark, they Steer with a Paddle, & row likewise with Paddles, they have Outlickers [outriggers] made of two spars & Boards laid on them, where to windward one or more sit to Balance the Boat

"the Double Canoes are very Large and are lashed together about two three or four feet asunder forward abaft & a Midships, they have two Masts which they Step between the two Canoes one forward & the other abaft &

their Shrouds are fixed to the outer Gunwale of each Canoe, they have large sails & are very Stiff — and go swift and live in a great Sea, they are about two feet & a half Broad within Board and the Plank of some of them at the Whole is above three inches, and at the gunwall about two, they are covered both forward and abaft for Eight or ten feet with Plank, & curved at each end so no water can come in but a Midships, they have likewais many of them large Square Rooms or Awnings fixed over both boats that will hold a Dozen People beside two or three on the Top, this Awning is fixed between the Two Masts."

As he pointed out in a later version of this report, there were three kinds of craft. The first were small canoes, carved from a single tree, which carried less than six people, and were used for fishing. All of these had an outrigger for balance. Then there were large double canoes, made of two hulls lashed together with two masts set up between them.

"With these vessels they sail far beyond the sight of land," he wrote, "probably to other islands, and bring home plantains, bananas, and yams, which seem also to be more plenty upon other parts of this island, than that off which the ship lay."

The third kind of canoe was "intended principally for pleasure and show: they are very large, but have no sail, and in shape resemble the gondolas of Venice: the middle is covered with a large awning, and some of the people sit upon it, some under it."

The fact that the "admiral" of the fleet that had attacked the *Dolphin* was on board one of this last type went unmentioned, as did the attack itself. Instead, Wallis launched himself into a description of the painstaking construction of these canoes, a long, arduous, and expert process, carried out with "the same exactness "that would be expected from an expert joiner."

The carefully fashioned planks were sewed in place with "a kind of plaited cordage," the gaps caulked with dried rushes, and the whole outside painted with a waterproof gum from their trees, which was every bit as good as pitch.

"we saw no kind of earthen ware amongs them," he went on, returning to more mundane matters; "their utensills were cocoaNutt Shells, Calibashes, wooden Trays neatly dug out & Basketts of diferent kinds in which they hung up their victualls at the Boughs of trees to keep the Rats from carrying it away

"the way they dress their meat is they make a large fire of cocoanutt Shells & wood, and leaves thrown over it to keep it from Blazing, when they think that the Stones are thoroughly Heated the take of the fire and brush the Stones very clean, then they take a small Hog wraped in Plantain leaves, or a larger cut in Quarters, and lay on the Stones and Yams wraped in Plantain leaves & fowles, & as much as they want to dress, on them they lay Breadfruit & Bananoes, & Plantains & other things that the mix up for eating all wrapt wraped up as the former, and on them they lay Plantain leaves all round then Cocoa nutt leaves, & after that the Embers and Coals of fire that was raked of on it the place Cocoa leaves, & close it well in and over with earth at least Six inches & let it remain 'till it is dressed [cooked]

"all of it is as well dressed as anything I ever tasted without being in the least burnt or dirty and full of gravy, the eat no kind of Sauce, neither did I see any Salt or vinager on any them but on Mr Furneaux first landing he found a small piece of salt Peter, but never saw any since.

"Sugar cane grows plenty, & some large, but the Natives make no other use of it than to Chew sometimes, they is great plenty of Sorrell like unto Clover in the Woods which our people eat of & had put in their Broth both for Breakfast & Dinner with the Breadfruit & Plantains."

As he described in a later version of his report, the Tahitians were astonished and impressed when they saw the gunner boil food in a pot, over a fire near his trading tent. "The iron pots which I afterwards gave to the queen, and several of the Chiefs" were used constantly from the moment they were received, "and brought as many people together, as a monster or a puppet-show in a country fair."

He had been glad to note that their only drink was water, and were "happily ignorant of the art of fermenting the juice of any vegetable, so as to give it an intoxicating quality." In fact, their only amusements seemed to be the arts of making love and making war. This last was very violent, it seemed, as some men had been carrying massive scars from wounds "made with stones, bludgeons, or some other obtuse weapon."

Because of this, Tahitian knowledge of medicine and surgery was surprisingly impressive. "One of our seamen, when he was on shore, run a large splinter into his foot," he described, going on to say that as the seaman was on shore, and the surgeon was on the ship, he had to get one of his shipmates to try to take it out with is penknife, "but after putting the poor fellow to a good deal of pain, was obliged to give it over.

"Our good old Indian, who happened to be present, then called over one of his countrymen that was standing on the opposite side of the river, who having looked at the seaman's foot, went immediately down to the beach, and taking up a shell, broke it to a point with his teeth; with this instrument, in little more than a minute, he laid open the place, and extracted the splinter."

Meantime, Fa'a had gone into the woods to extract some gum from an "apple" tree, "which he applied to the wound upon a piece of the cloth that was wrapped round him, and in two days time it was perfectly healed."

Wallis had made sure to do some measuring, no doubt with the myth of the "Patagonian giants" in his mind. "The inhabitants of this island are a stout, well-made, active and comely people," he wrote in a later version of this report. "The stature of the men, in general, is from five feet seven to five feet ten inches, though a few individuals are taller, and a few shorter; that of the women from five feet to five feet six."

The women were also "extremely beautiful. Chastity does not seem to be considered as a virtue among them," he meditated in his draft, "for they not only readily and openly trafficked with our people for personal favours, but were brought down by their fathers and brothers for that purpose: they were, however, conscious of the value of beauty, and the size of the nail that was demanded for the enjoyment of the lady, was always in proportion to her charms."

There was a method to the bargaining, as he went on to reveal. "The men who came down to the side of the river, at the same time that they presented the girl, shewed a stick of the size of the nail that was to be her price, and if our people agreed, she was sent over to them."

This was because the men were not supposed to cross the river, the officers being told to keep a strict watch. Not that it made any difference, as "while some straggled a little way to receive the lady," their shipmates kept a sharp look out. "When I was acquainted with it, I no longer wondered that the ship was in danger of being pulled to pieces for the nails and iron that held her together."

This led to another reflection — that the worthies in the Admiralty might accuse the *Dolphin* of introducing venereal disease to the island, a possibility that he hastily denied, though with very shaky logic.

"It is certain that none of our people contracted the venereal disease here," he wrote, "and therefore, as they had free commerce with great numbers of the women, there is the greatest probability that it was not then known in the country."

So, if it did not exist in Tahiti before they arrived, and his men were all hale and hearty when they sailed, the disease could not have been brought to the island by the *Dolphin*.

Or so he reckoned.

# Chapter 12:
## "Towards old England"

*At Noon, Port Royal Harbour being the Name I gave*
*the Port we Sailed from Bore SE½E Distance about*
*Twelve Miles — Served fresh Pork to the Ships Company*
*who thank God are all healthy and well, myself and two*
*Lieutenants being the only Invalids, and we in a*
*recovering way tho' excessive low and weak*

— Wallis, journal on the *Dolphin*, July 27, 1767

Within a week of departure from Tahiti, the *Dolphin* lost
a sailor — the first man to die on the voyage. On August 1,
Wallis wrote, "William Welch Seaman fell of the Main
Yard on the Ship Gunwall & broke himself to pieces &
dyed at Ten in the Morn."

George Robertson, like everyone else, was shocked,
saying, "He was a very Sober diligent young man, and
hade the General esteem of all the Officers." Accordingly,
there was general relief when another bout of rough
weather did not lead to more deaths. One man fell
overboard, and saved himself by grabbing one of the
captain's chairs, which had been thrown into the water,
while another man who fell onto the deck from aloft
escaped with bad bruising.

On 12 August, two islands were raised. "The first of
these I Named Boscawen's Isle — The Second Keppel's

Island," wrote Wallis. He sent George Robertson with a boat's party to scout for an anchoring place, and claim the group for King George, while the ship tacked back and forth. The master arrived back with mixed news. He could find no anchorage, but the natives were willing to trade fruit and coconuts, so the ship lingered while their stocks were replenished.

Two days later another small island was raised, clothed in coconut trees. It was part of a small group, and supported about forty inhabitants, who would trade nothing. "Mr Clarke & the rest of the Officers of the Ship did me the Honour to call this Island after my Name," wrote Wallis.

Unlike all the other places he named during the voyage, which have all reverted to the way they were known before he arrived, this atoll group — though, ironically, French territory — is still known as "the Wallis Islands."

After negotiating the passage between Tonga and Samoa (where, lacking a native interpreter on board, as no Tahitians had volunteered to come to England, he had no meaningful dealings with the islanders), Wallis shaped his course northwest for the island of Tinian, in the northern Marianas. Throughout this passage through the western Pacific, he sailed as fast as he could without risking undue damage to his ship or canvas, being acutely aware that within six weeks of running out of fresh provisions, the first signs of scurvy would appear in his men.

Because they were headed to the East Indies, it was doubly dangerous. Not only was scurvy a killer in itself, but the rash that heralded the horrible malady would bring with it weakness, weariness, and a lack of resistance to other diseases—diseases like dysentery and malaria, which were endemic to the South China Sea. The *Dolphin* fetched the island of Tinian in September, and the anchor was dropped on the nineteenth. Immediately after the ship was snug, Wallis devoted his attention to the crewmen who were showing symptoms of scurvy.

Only one man — seaman William Welch, the man who had taken a fatal tumble from the mainyard — had died in the course of the long, stormy passage, but the sickbay was full. Hands were sent on shore to collect coconuts and oranges, and pitch tents ready to receive the invalids, and there the ship stayed for the next month, with Surgeon John Hutchinson in command of the makeshift hospital.

While the ship was being thoroughly overhauled, the *Dolphin*s feasted on poultry, limes, breadfruit, oranges and pawpaw, plus the fresh beef that John Gore, who was in charge of a hunting party (and signed off his journal with the words "Master hunter"), sent to the beach from the jungles of the interior. There were no inhabitants to trouble them, as the Spanish had moved everyone to Guam, so apart from the hordes of flies, the thick, almost impenetrable brambles, and the uncertainty of the anchorage (they lost one anchor when the cable was cut by a rock), Wallis was able to rest and relax as he watched his men recover their health.

Finally, on October 16, 1767, he wrote, "I came onboard with all the People Tents &c the Ship being compleat with everything that could be got here at 6 am weighed and stood to the North End of the Island, sent the Boats onshoar and brought of Mr Gore & his Party, with a Bullock."

After taking his departure from Tinian, Wallis felt his way through the South China Sea to Batavia (modern Jakarta), following Byron's charts and constantly checking his navigational calculations. The weather was squally, with thunderstorms, and at midnight on October 29, in rough weather, the *Dolphin* lost her second man - a marine "taylor" by the name of Edmund Morgan fell overboard while drunk.

The ship dropped anchor at Batavia on December 1, 1767 — "Sent an Officer to the Governor to acquaint him of the arrival of his Brittanick Maj:ˢ Ship Dolphin," noted Wallis, "& that we might be permitted to furnish the ship with such necessaries as we wanted, that we would Salute if he would return an Equal Number of Guns from the fort onshoar, that being agreed to, at Sunrise Saluted with 13 Guns, the Fort returned 13 Guns."

Going on shore, he took one horrified look at the fetid, mosquito-infested canals meandering through the town, and came back to issue orders that no one should be allowed on shore, except on essential business. He sailed again just six days later, "All the people in good health," having refused to purchase any of the rotten provisions on offer.

Instead, he steered for Prince's Island, an island at the western entrance of Sunda Strait, to refresh the ship's store of firewood, trade for turtle, and try to do something about the "Ratts, which are so plenty in the Ship that they distroy Sails Rigging Provisions & the Peoples Clothes."

Four days after they arrived, he noted, "Benjamin Lad fell from the mainyard into a Boat alongside and hurt himself terribly & bruized two other men in the Boat that he fell partly on." Ladd survived, but John Wooldridge, one of the seamen who had cushioned his fall, suffered a lingering death from internal injuries.

It was not the end of bad news. Wallis took his departure for the Cape of Good Hope on December 20, 1767, and three days later, "George Lewis Quarter Master" terrified them all by dying in the middle of a violent fit.

Four days after that, he was followed by "John Bowden Seaman", who had been sick of some stomach complaint (perhaps cancer) for a long time.

Meantime, disease had come on board, despite the precautions taken at Batavia. "Severall people taken ill of Fevers & Fluxes," wrote Wallis; "and they seem much cast down which I believe is owing to the damp air for the Ship is very clean & the sick have everything they could wish."

Getting into the fresher air of the Indian Ocean did not help. The new year dawned with thirty-seven men confined to the sickbay, and by January 6, 1768 there were forty on the sick list, including the surgeon's mate — "makes it fall heavy on the Surgeon, whose humanity will scarce allow him scarce a single moment's rest."

To cope, Captain Wallis made alterations to his ship — "cleared a very large Berth for the sick and separated them from the rest of the Ship's Crew." Those seamen and marines who were still fit to work were shifted to the half-deck — the area aft of the mainmast, under the awning — and the berth deck was turned into a seaborne hospital.

This was hung with painted canvas, which was washed with vinegar — "this Birth is kept exceeding Clean and washed every morning with vinegar, and fumigated with Pitch burning." The fumigation was carried out by a man walking through the berth with a shovel of burning sulphur. Drinking water was sterilized by plunging "a dagger made red hot" into it, and instead of beer or grog, the patients were given wine from the captain's own stores.

"They have saloup every morning for Breakfast or sagoe (the Surgeon having laid in a great quantity)," Wallis wrote, "saloup" being a glutinous gruel made from the roots of a species of orchid, which was very much in

129

vogue at the time as a medication for invalids. Incredibly, only one man died: "Joseph Gilson Marine Departed this Life" on January 12, 1768.

Thirty-nine men who would have otherwise died lived to see England again, which was a testament not just to Dr John Hutchinson's dedication to his patients, but to his methods, too. The report Wallis asked him to write two days before arriving home (and which was given to James Cook to be carried on the *Endeavour*), described his treatment of fever with a light diet (which included honey as well as "saloop"), augmented "with frequent distributions to the sick from the Captain's table."

Crucially, because of Wallis's insistence on plenty of fresh provisions, cleanliness, and sufficient time off for sleep, there was no scurvy on board, and the men had good natural resistance.

*Shipping at the Cape of Good Hope*
From *The Neptune Library*

The ship made port at the Cape of Good Hope on February 5, 1768. Dropping anchor should have brought relief, but the surgeon came back from his first shore-side visit to report that "the Smallpox was all over the Town." Accordingly, Wallis arranged for a camp to be set up in a secluded field on a point of open land, and the sick were sent there, with the surgeon to care for them. The rest of the crew were allowed on shore, turn and turn about, and greens and fresh meat were served daily to all.

By February 11, "our Sick People recover fast," he wrote, "and have kept themselves very orderly, the Midshipmen prevent any of the Inhabitants coming to them, it being two miles from the Town, & an Open pleasant Spot." The ploy was outstandingly successful. On March 3, 1768, he was able to take his departure for England, with everyone on board and in good health.

And, while he had lost men to accident and disease, not a single man had died of scurvy. It was a remarkable accomplishment — and one that history has neglected to recognize.

# Chapter 13:
## "Ship News Extraordinary"

"½ past 4 Anchored in the Downs", noted Wallis in his deck log on May 19, 1768. Deal Castle was in sight, and the ship was just one and a half miles from shore. "Got the Sheet Anchor over the Side" he concluded, and after signing the page, he closed the logbook. Then he took a boat to the landing place, where he hired a horse to take him to London and the Admiralty, carrying his charts, Dr Hutchinson's letter, and the journals he had collected.

Left in charge, Lieutenant Clarke supervised the drying of the mildewed sails, and the scrubbing of the weatherworn hull and decks, waiting for the "Clerk of the Cheque" to inspect the men and pass the muster. His instructions from Wallis had been to stop the men from talking about the island they had discovered, but instead, when the man from Lloyds arrived, they crowded at the rail, keen to talk.

Not only did they have a grand new word — "tattoo" — to add to the English vocabulary, but they had amazing tales to tell: of bare-breasted, remarkably generous girls; of a country where no one had to work, as food could be plucked off the trees; of chiefs robed like Roman senators; and of an open-hearted island queen. It also seems that George Robertson, the sailing master, may have given —

or sold — a written account of the discovery of Tahiti to the reporter.

Because of guaranteed public interest, the newspaperman's first questions were about the giant Patagonians. He received tongue in cheek answers to that, because the Irish *Public Advertiser, or Freeman's Journal,* reported on 21 May that the *Dolphin* had thirteen Patagonians on board, which would be landed at Greenwich. Then the focus of attention switched fast, as tales of "a large, fertile and extremely populous Island in the South-Sea" were spun.

On May 23, *Lloyd's Evening Post* broke the news to a breathless public that the *Dolphin*s had found "a large, fertile, and extremely populous Island" in the South Seas. "From the Behaviour of the Inhabitants, we had Reason to believe she was the first and only Ship they had ever seen," the writer declared, going on to impart the salacious detail that the Tahitian maidens "endeavoured to engage the Attention of our Sailors, by exposing their beauties to their view."

The attack on the ship was described, along with the "disagreeable Necessity" of quelling this rebellion with cannon balls and grapeshot, creating such devastation that the islanders "now looked on our People as more than human." The Tahitians bore no umbrage for the slaughter, because they were intelligent enough to realize "that we had only made use of those dreadful Engines against them when their Rashness had forced us to it."

Nor did they seem to resent the appropriation of their country, and its rechristening as "KING GEORGE'S LAND." Much space was devoted to the "Queen," whose husband had been killed in the attack, but who nonetheless became so fond of the interlopers that "the last Thing she did was to take the Crown from her own Head, and present it to Capt. Wallace. It has been carefully preserved," the writer went on; "and is to be presented to her Majesty of Great Britain."

All of the London newspapers reprinted the story, there being no copyright law in those days. In July it reached as far as Scotland, where it was published in the thirtieth edition of *Scots Magazine*.

"The *Dolphin* man of war, Capt. Wallis, arrived in the Thames about the 20th of May from another voyage round the world," the item began. "A new island is said to have been discovered by them in the South Seas, large, fertile, and extremely populous – The following account is given of it by one of the people on board—

> *We came to an anchor in a safe, spacious and commodious harbour, where we lay about six weeks. From the behaviour of the inhabitants, we had reason to believe we were the first and only ship they had ever seen.*

> *The first day they came along-side on a number of canoes, in order to take possession of our ship. There were two divisions, one filled with men, and the other with women. These last endeavoured to engage the attentions of our sailors by exposing their beauties to their view, while the men from the canoes threw great quantities of stones, by which several seamen were hurt. – However, as they had no kind of weapons, they were soon beat off, and a few vollies of firearms obliged them to retire in great confusion.*

> *The day following a party well armed was sent on shore with the water casks; and our people at the topmast head, discovered, by the help of their glasses, prodigious numbers of the natives flocking from all parts towards*

135

*the watering place, in order to surround the party: upon which a signal was made for them to come on board, and leave the watering casks.*

*This was no sooner done, than the Dolphin was attacked by greater numbers than the day preceding; which reduced us to the disagreeable necessity of firing some of our great guns at them, charged with grape-shot; and some guns with ball were also fired up the country, which knocked down some of their houses, felled several trees, &c. And strock them with such awe, that they now looked on our people as more than human, since their houses could not shelter them, nor distance take them out of reach of our shot.*

*They then showed the greatest desire of being at peace with us, and did not seem to resent the killing a number of their people, as they now appeared to be sensible, that we had only made use of those dreadful engines against them when their rashness forced us to it.*

*We took possession of the island in His Majesty's name, and called it KING GEORGE'S LAND. It lies about twenty degrees southern latitude. During the remainder of our stay, we continued to trade with the natives in the same amicable manner, giving them nails, buttons, beads and trinkets in exchange for fresh provisions, which we were greatly in want of.*

*The natives are in general taller and stouter made than our people; and are mostly of a copper colour, with black hair; others are fairer, especially the women, some of whom we observed to be red-haired. – It does not appear that they know the use of anyone metal whatever. – When the grape-shot came among them, they dived after it, and brought up the pieces of lead. They swim like fish, and can remain a long time under water.*

– They were cloathed with a kind of stuff made from the bark of trees, some red, some yellow; its texture resembles that of coarse thick paper, and cannot resist wet. Besides the large island, there are several other ones, which have been amed Charlotte Island, Gloucester Island, Boscawen's Island, Keppel Island, Wallis Island, &c.

The island to which was given the name of King George's land, was governed by a Queen, to whom the natives seemed to pay the utmost reverence, as they obeyed not only her words, but even her looks and gestures. She expressed the most lively sorrow on our leaving the island; and the last thing she did, was to take the crown from her own head, and present it to Capt. Wallis. It has been carefully preserved, and is to be presented to her Majesty of G. Britain.

The inhabitants of the new discovered island are pretty much civilized, considering that the arts have made but little progress among them, and that they are unacquainted with the use of any metals, not even of iron. From some circumstances, we had reason to imagine, that the King of the island was killed in the attack on the second day: the Queen was cloathed in red, which we found was the mourning of the country

– 'Tis impossible to describe the beautiful prospects we beheld in this charming spot; the verdure is as fine as that of England, there is great plenty of live stock, and it abounds with all the choicest productions of the earth.

Two days after the story first appeared in print, on Wednesday, May 25, the pilot arrived on board the ship, the anchors were weighed, and the *Dolphin* began her upriver passage. At noon on May 29, she arrived at the Royal Naval Docks in Deptford — commonly known as "King's Yard" - to be directed to a mooring alongside HMS *Surprise*.

A 24-gun sixth-rater with a record of capturing a half-dozen enemy privateers in the past war, *Surprise's* measurements were so close to those of the *Dolphin* she could have been a sister ship. This, for the *Dolphins*, was rather depressing, as the other frigate was about to be sold out of the service.

All about them commotion reigned, harsh to ears accustomed to breezes in the rigging and the hiss of the sea. The King's Yard was a conglomeration of slipways and basins, piers for fitting out, lines of sheds, tall rigging houses, and long sail-lofts. Timber for masts and yards floated in shallow rectangular pools of brine.

Loud hammering sounded from unseen forges, accompanied by the shouts of shipwrights and carpenters, the tap-tapping of coopering, rattling chains, ropes splashing into the water, and even the bleating of goats. A sweet smell of ship's biscuit wafted from the shoreside bakeries, mingling with the sulfurous reek of smoke and the resinous sting of tar.

Beyond, the scene was even more compelling, familiar and yet foreign for men who remembered the volcanic peaks and forests of Tahiti. Past the grand buildings that rimmed the cluttered grounds, the reflections of East Pond and West Pond shimmered in the sky. To the west stretched immense gardens, where vegetables for the London markets were raised.

Farther up the river lay the dock where the Greenland whalemen discharged their oil (and where the mouth of the creek was guarded by dolphins, or so the sailors said), and farther still, beyond the thickets of masts in the inner pool of the Thames, lay a city of more than 600,000 inhabitants, crowding the horizon with spires and domes.

There was a great deal of work to be done before the crew could be disbanded. Sails were unbent, running rigging unreeved, and yards and topmasts unrigged and sent down. Stores that had not been used during the voyage had to be hoisted out of the hold and onto the wharf.

In the morning the men had a break, being given permission to go "onshore to refresh." It was early. As they strolled through the tortuous alleys, past tenements, slaughter-houses, and breweries, the malodorous air rang with the shouted pleadings of street-mongers, the clanging bells of dustmen and scavengers - and the trumpets blown by the newspaper vendors.

By now, almost everyone in London knew the story.

Within days, the ship was paid off. On 10 June 1768, Wallis made the note: "At 10 AM came down the Commis'd and paid off the ship & struck the Pennant," and signed it, "Sam¹ Wallis." He was now unemployed, with a £500 gratuity. His men fared even worse - on average, they received just £24 for two years' work. Their only gain from the long, dangerous voyage was a fund of tales.

As Wallis noted on the last page of his old logbook, the *Dolphin*s penned a petition, which they gave to him with a polite request to carry it to the Admiralty. "We should not have dared to have made thus bold with you, had we not been encouraged by the Humane and generous treatment we have so often experienced since we have had the happiness to be commanded by you," the letter began.

Then, after expressing their deep gratitude, vowing and declaring he was their "only Prop" in these uncertain times, the sailors came to the point:

> *We humbly beg that you may recommend us to their Lordships favor as it is certain that thro your goodness in so doing must depend our Good or bad fortunes and as we came out in a state of uncertainty, makes us that bold to solicit you in our behalf—*

Samuel Wallis copied the petition into his old logbook, and put the original in his pocket, in preparation for a meeting with their Lordships.

With a party of sailors, he proceeded up the river in the ship's boats to Whitehall Stairs, then marched to the Admiralty at the head of a small procession, bearing trophies of the *Dolphin*'s trailblazing voyage. A band of weathered seamen shouldered a fishing canoe stolen from Queen Charlotte Island (Nukutavake, in the Tuamotus), after the islanders had fled. Another mahogany-tanned party was loaded with bales of Tahitian tapa, while more carried boxes holding Purea's gifts, including the wreaths of hair and tufts of sacred feathers, destined to be presented to Queen Charlotte.

Two men had boxes of seeds collected by Furneaux and Gore, which were eventually passed on to the Royal Botanic Gardens at Kew. More sailors carried Tahitian artifacts - a drum, a "spontoon" (a kind of halberd), a flute, a "Conque," breastplates, a "Bow & Casquette of Arrows," fish and shark hooks, "Instruments for marking their backsides," a fishing net, and "a stone for bruizing their bread," all of which, with the Nukutavake canoe, and some "oars found on Osnaburg Island" (Maitea), were in due course presented to the museum.

What their Lordships of the Admiralty really wanted was the paperwork of the voyage, which Wallis himself was carrying: "Draughts and perspective views," his journal "with all courses steered, weather & remarks" (these last written by Robertson), and "a Book of all the Observations of Longitude as Observed by Mr. Maskelines Tables - with one Observation of an Eclipse which hapned while we were at Georges Island."

All of this was going to prove very useful indeed. Because of the precise observations made by the talented John Harrison, purser of the *Dolphin*, and the charts of Matavai Bay made by Robertson and his mates, Lieutenant James Cook, just appointed to the command of the *Endeavour* expedition, now had a precise location to steer for, and a known place to set up an observatory and record the transit of Venus.

The *Dolphins*' petition got a chillier reception. As *Scots Magazine* reported in a single convoluted sentence:

> *London, June 24: The seamen who went round the world in the Dolphin man of war in her last voyage, and who had petitioned the King for an additional pay, were ordered to attend the admiralty for an answer; and on Thursday fo'night, we are informed, a few of them, who were deputed by the whole body, attend, with the master of that ship; when they were told, that if they would serve on board the guardships at the different ports, suitable notice would be taken of them with respect to promotion; but that, with regard to any additional pay, Capt. Wallis was told before he sailed, that no such*

*encouragement would be given; that although they
quoted Commodore Byron's voyage as a precedent, yet it
argued nothing in their favour, since the undertaking at
that time, was deemed a desperate one had having
neither charts, maps, or authentic directions for
governing himself by, nor were the officers and people in
the least apprised of the undertaking; while, on the
contrary, those who went on the second voyage, had not
only the materials, such as the charts, maps, and logbooks, of the first voyage, as well as a pilot, who had been
on that voyage; but that all them were well acquainted at
the time they imbarked, that their enterprise was
intended for the South Sea. These arguments, we hear,
have had the desired effect.*

"I gave it to the first Lord of the Admiralty who said it
did me great Honour," Wallis noted in his old logbook,
adding with palpable bitterness, "and this was all either
they or I got by the Voyage but much ill health & fatigue."

And so they all dispersed, so widely that the fates of
just a few are known.

John Gore, the stalwart master's mate who served as a
deck officer, head of the wooding party, and "master
hunter" at Tinian, joined Cook's *Endeavour* as third
lieutenant. Three other *Dolphin* hands kept him company
on this voyage back to Tahiti, where they proved very
useful, having a smattering of the language, and being able
to recognize some of the important people there - Tupaia
and "the Queen," in particular.

One was Richard Pickersgill, who, despite his age (just nineteen) was considered experienced enough to be enlisted as a master's mate. And the master himself was twenty-two-year-old Molineux. The fourth was the promising Frank Wilkinson, who embarked on the *Endeavour* as an able seaman, though he was soon to be promoted to master's mate, too.

Tobias Furneaux, the lieutenant who had claimed Tahiti in the name of the king, was ill for some time after the voyage, but recovered in time to command the *Adventure* on Cook's second expedition. This time, he entered the Pacific on the Cape of Good Hope route, and accordingly became the first man to sail around the world in both directions.

The absence of George Robertson from the crewlist of the *Endeavour* is notable, particularly as not only had he navigated throughout, and kept a good record of his calculations, but he had trained three of the old *Dolphin*s who were given berths. He was still on the *Dolphin*, in charge of the anchored frigate as shipkeeper, though it seems likely he applied for a post on the *Endeavour*, as in 1771 he wrote a letter to Banks, begging him to find him a position on the *Resolution*.

He had a black mark on his record, as not only had he led the *Dolphin*s' protest, but it was obviously he who defied orders by talking to the reporters. Instead of joining the *Endeavour* expedition, as a kind of sop he was promoted to the rank of third lieutenant, and his pay for this back-dated to June 1, 1766 — with the proviso that he passed the examination before the Board first. This he did, and duly became second lieutenant of the *Aquilon*.

A couple of posts later, as an officer on *Peggy* in 1769, and then on *Namur* — plus a couple of years of sick leave in New York — he was given the command of the *Phoenix*, and took part in the patrol of the North American coast, then played a lively role in the Revolutionary War, transporting troops and seizing cattle.

In July 1778 he took command of the *Dependance*, still on the coast of New England. Finally, in July 1779, he was discharged to the *Ardent*, and there his record ends.

Samuel Wallis, despite his precarious health, continued his navy career. In 1770, during Britain's dispute with Spain over the ownership of the Falkland Islands, he took command of the man of war *Torbay*, moving on to the quarterdeck of the *Dublin*. Finally, in October 1782, he resigned from active service to become an extra commissioner of the navy, a post he still held in 1795.

But, in the meantime, there had been much to remind him of the discovery of Tahiti.

# Chapter 14:  The Unfortunate Compiler

The *Dolphin*s did not have the monopoly of spicy revelations for very long. In April 1768, one month before the *Dolphin* got home, two French exploring ships had dropped anchor off the eastern coast of Tahiti, and, though the French sailors and scientists stayed for just nine days, they carried away the same tales of a pastoral paradise, complete with willing golden girls.

According to Louis de Bougainville, the commander of the expedition, Tahiti was a utopia "worthy of the paintbrush of Boucher," an enchanted isle where "nymphs" would drop their draperies without a blush, and Venus was the goddess of hospitality. These revelations created a sensation in Paris, helped by the presence of the real, live Tahitian Bougainville brought home with him, a husky and attractive young chief by the name of Ahutoru. This young and confident fellow had boarded a French ship the moment he could reach her with a canoe, and was so familiar with European customs and dress that he could very well have been the same young man who had been nicknamed "Jonathan" by the officers of the *Dolphin*.

Still more salacious tales, told by the complement of the *Endeavour*, were in the offing. In March 1769, when de Bougainville arrived home with his enticing tales, the *Endeavour* was just days away from dropping anchor at

Matavai Bay. There, Cook's sailors, being "rich in iron," having fitted themselves out with spikes and nails before leaving Plymouth Dockyard, ranged on shore with randy delight.

Their assistant surgeon, William Perry, reminisced that "two spikes and one looking-glass" would procure "the most fastidious" and the most beautiful, even a lady-in-waiting to the queen — "What were the joyous exertions on the part of my shipmates on such an Island, I leave to imagination!"

Up until 1771, the Tahitian tales were just tavern gossip and newspaper items, but then the *Endeavour* returned to England, with young Joseph Banks on board. The handsome young man became the instant Lion of London, in demand in salons and clubs everywhere, because of the many bawdy and rousing tales he told so well. And so, impressed by the huge public interest in Tahiti that Banks had inspired, Lord Sandwich, First Lord of the Admiralty, decided to commission a freelance writer by the name of John Hawkesworth to write a popular account of the voyage.

It was an odd choice, as Hawkesworth was a literary hack with only one great talent, that of cultivating useful friends. A great admirer of Samuel Johnson, he emulated his style, flattering the great man so much that he was chosen to succeed Johnson as the compiler of parliamentary debates for the *Gentleman's Magazine*. Then, with Johnson, he founded a periodical, *The Adventurer*, which was so lofty in tone that the Archbishop of Canterbury rewarded him with an honorary doctorate. Significantly, he also had success with classical tales and eastern fairy stories, which snared him a commission to write dramas for David Garrick. And, because of this last, he became friendly with Garrick's musical collaborator, Charles Burney, incidentally the father of the James Burney who sailed with Cook.

In September 1771, when Lord Sandwich was casting around for someone to write the book he had in mind, Burney introduced him to Hawkesworth, saying that not only was he a good fellow, but he had the time to write up the account, and could certainly do with the money. It seems the two men were most compatible — within weeks, the First Lord was writing teasingly to Hawkesworth, saying, "That I may be certain whether you are alive or dead, I shall be obliged to you if you will either come yourself or send your ghost to dine with me tomorrow. I am most sincerely yours, Sandwich."

And so Hawkesworth snared the commission, and immediately sold the publication rights to the publishers Strahan and Cadell, for the immense sum of six thousand pounds — the equivalent of £750,000, or $3,750,000, today. What Sandwich thought of this is unknown, but it triggered a mood of such virulent jealousy in the literary arena that John Hawkesworth may well have regretted it later.

Unknowing, meantime, he set to the task with a will. It was a huge challenge, as it had been decided to include the voyages of Byron, Carteret, and Wallis, as well as that of Cook, but Hawkesworth completed the first two volumes of the three-volume set in just four months.

He began by requisitioning the journals kept by all four captains, plus those kept by Joseph Banks and George Robertson. Providentially, the *Dolphin*'s old sailing master was available, as he had just been paid off from his position of sixth lieutenant on the ship-of-the-line *Namur*. This was lucky for Wallis (who was also handy, having been paid off from HMS *Torbay* when she had made port in Plymouth), as all he had was his sketchy logbook, which

147

was woefully incomplete in many parts, because he had been so ill.

Consulting with his erstwhile sailing master, he turned the logbook into a much more complete journal — one which, naturally, presented his actions in the best light possible. Then — after having a copy made, he being a careful and prudent man — he handed it over to Hawkesworth, who mined it thoroughly, writing penciled notes in the margins.

Probably in imitation of his old captain, though it also might have been because he enjoyed writing and reminiscing so much, Robertson turned his own logbook into a racy journal, including sexual adventures that he coyly described as happening to "my friend," though it is obvious that he was telling naughty tales about himself. This was used by Hawkesworth, too, as it had the kind of material that the writer was looking for, the sort of titillating stuff that would guarantee public interest and lots of sales, so there are pencilled notations in the same hand as those in the Wallis public journal. And then, with boundless energy and enthusiasm, Hawkesworth set to writing up the *Dolphin*'s voyage and events in Tahiti, by editing what Samuel Wallis and George Robertson had given him, and adding a few anecdotes they had told him, too.

Hawkesworth was not the most honorable of editors. Back in 1755, when he had edited the letters of Jonathan Swift, a lot of the so-called "editing" had turned out to be blatant rewriting. And obviously, if he felt free to tinker with the prose of such a great author, rewriting the words of rough sailors was going to be a breeze – and his brief was to produce a book that appealed to the wider public, not the intelligentsia, which gave him a lot of freedom.

Accordingly, Wallis's "Oberea" became "my princess, or rather, queen," and the scene inside the *fare hau* at the time of the first visit included an amusing anecdote about the Tahitians' stunned reaction when the sweating surgeon took off his wig — a story that Hawkesworth either made up or learned in conversation, as it is not in Wallis's journal. The massage by the Tahitian maidens was drawn out sensuously, having obvious appeal, and the titillating tidbit about the girls having difficulty in dressing the men again was added.

Being personally clothed "according to the fashion of the country" by the queen herself appealed to the reader's imagination, too, completed by the image of her tenderly lifting Wallis over the muddy patches on the way back to the landing. And finally, the heartbreaking scenes of the queen's distress when Captain Wallis insisted on leaving the island merited a lot more lingering prose.

The three-volume *Account of the Voyages Undertaken by the Order of His Present Majesty ... by Commodore Byron, Captain Wallis, Captain Carteret and Captain Cook, in the Dolphin, the Swallow, and the Endeavour...* was an instant bestseller. Even at the vast price of three guineas, the first print run of 2,000 sets sold out within weeks, and a second print of 2,500 was produced two months later. It was one of the most popular books of the century, borrowed from libraries hundreds of times.

This was partly because of the enduring public fascination with books of travel and adventure, but much was due to its coyly sensuous tone and sly hints about Wallis's true relationship with his "princess, or rather, queen" — something that the reviewers leapt on. As the critic for the *Gentleman's Magazine* mused in the throes of a very long and uncharitable review, by the time the ship

149

had been at the island for a month, "they had not only found means of being reconciled to the inhabitants, but of being caressed by them.

"The girls were still fond of nails, and even the Queen had her longings. There was not a nail or spike inside or out of the ship, that the sailors could get at, but was drawn; and the Captain, to prevent the ship from being pulled to pieces, was obliged to issue orders, that no man should go ashore without special leave. The Queen, however, made frequent visits on board, and was as frequently visited on shore by the Captain."

The reviewer also seized on the "Indian" Queen's "excess of passion" when Wallis insisted that the ship must leave. "The writer of the voyage has very pathetically described the parting of the Captain and his Indian Queen," he wrote. "It is so very similar to that of Dido and Aeneas, in the IVth book of Virgil, that we are apt to suspect him indebted to the poet for some of the tenderest strokes."

He was not the only one to liken this "excess of passion" to the despair of Dido, Queen of Carthage, when she was abandoned by the Trojan hero, Aeneas. Another was Horace Walpole. "Dr Hawkesworth is still more provoking," he wrote to his friend, the Countess of Ossory, on June 21, 1773:

> An old black gentlewoman of forty carries Captain Wallis across a river, when he was too weak to walk, and the man represents them as a new edition of Dido and Aeneas. Indeed, Dido the new does not even borrow the obscurity of a cave when she treats the travelers with the rites of Love, as practiced in Otaheite

150

Other reviews were even more vicious. The work was attacked for pomposity, inaccuracy, its lewdness and its impiety. It was an example, as one blustered, of "the maxim that those who are destitute of the fundamental principles of religion and morality will grasp at gold with avidity."

They say that bad reviews do not kill, but it seems very possible that the hail of acrimony contributed to Hawkesworth's death. He passed away of a "slow fever," the same year as the wok was published, on 17 November 1773.

But Wallis lived on, to bear the brunt of the salacious rumors that persisted.

The next shock for Wallis, and probably a greater one, was a long ballad, called *The Injured Islanders,* which was published anonymously in 1779. Again, it was inspired by the legend of Dido and Aeneas.

Illustrated with sentimental etchings, it was a plea from the "queen" — "faithful OBRA" — to Samuel Wallis — "illustrious WALLIS!" — begging him to return to her arms, and repair the plunge in her fortunes that had happened since he had left. As the writer pointed out in the preface, being discovered by Europeans had done the Tahitians no good at all.

No other book had "afforded more Entertainment to the Public than the late Voyages to the Southern Ocean," he meditated; "their Design, and the Degree of Success that has attended it are now generally known: But whatever Advantages either the Spirit of Enterprize, or commercial and scientific Interests may derive from some Discoveries that have been made in that distant Hemisphere, it is much to be lamented, that the innocent Natives have been sufferers by the Event." And the Queen was a particular sufferer.

THE

# INJURED ISLANDERS;

OR,

## THE INFLUENCE OF ART

UPON

## THE HAPPINESS OF NATURE.

LONDON,

PRINTED FOR J. MURRAY, No. 32, OPPOSITE ST. DUNSTAN'S CHURCH,
FLEET-STREET.

MDCCLXXIX.

Since the advent of the Europeans, Oberea had been stripped "of that Wealth and Power which so eminently distinguished her at Captain WALLIS'S arrival," and now she cried for help:

> Thy fervent Vows in Friendship's Guise array'd
> While more than friendship ev'ry Vow convey'd —
> These all recurring, constant as the Day,
> Reign in my Breast resistless in their Sway,
> Usurp the Scenes my free-born Pleasures knew,
> Nor leave a Wish unleagu'd with Love and You.
>
> Late, as along the Verdure-vested Lawn
> My Morning Steps approach'd the blushing Dawn,
> Far from the Beach, and pendent from the Sky,
> A distant Vessel caught my longing Eye;
> The purple Streamers, Wave by Waves, appear,
> And Love still whispers, lo! Thy WALLIS near;
> Oh joyful Hope! — to greet Thee I prepare,
> And bind the TOMOU round my fragrant Hair,
> With grateful Gifts of vegetable Store
> I haste impatient to the crowded Shore:
> In vain I haste — no WALLIS meets me there,
> No Friend, no Fondness to reward my Care.
>
> Bereft of power, and destitute of Train,
> My humble Off'ring scarce Acceptance gain
> To richer Chiefs, who rule TAHEITEE'S Land,
> The British Treasures pass from Hand to Hand,
> The Crimson Plumes, the Beads of brightest Die,
> The Mirrors faithful to the Gazer's eye,
> The precious Gifts, whose boasted Aid we feel,
> Of pointed Iron, and of polish'd Steel —
> Boast tho' we may, to judge them by the past,
> These Gifts may prove our fatal Foes at last.

By piercing Steel tho' proudest Forests fall,
And take new forms at Man's Imperial Call,
By Steel too Man his Fellow Man annoys,
It tempts as Plunder, and as Death destroys;
The dang'rous Wealth exotic Wants inspires
Where equal Nature levell'd all Desires,
And, social Freedom sapped by envious Strife,
We risk at once our Morals and our Life.

Curs'd the Desire for Wealth like this that made
A rival Chief my royal Realms invade!
The lifted Ax — Ah! WALLIS, shall I tell?
On our Friends with dreadful Havock fell ...

O Thou, in whom my Heart still seeks Repose,
Haste to prevent, or mitigate our Woes;
O WALLIS, haste, and, emulous of Praise
Our drooping Spirits to their Level raise,
Till native Joys, the Mists of Error past,
Again return, and brighten to the last.

Canst thou forget? Can Memory e'er betray
The last sad Hour I urged your longer Stay?
The Masts were rear'd with Arms extended wide
To scourge the Storm and awe th'insurgent Tide,
While, fondly flutt'ring to the favourite Gale,
Rose the fair Bosom of the swelling Sail;
Back to the Beach, desponding still, and slow,
I vainly turn'd to shun the coming Woe,
No Shark-tooth Punctures pour'd a sanguine Stream,
But Heart-sprung Sorrows flooded all my frame,
Till my faint Soul in silent Anguish fell,
Rose but in Sighs, and feebly breath'd — farewell!

154

Touch'd with my Grief, and friendly to my Fears,
 Midst the broad Deck you mark'd the circling Years,
On sacred Plumes this solemn vow express'd,
To Heav'n and me alternately address'd,
That ere the splendid rule of the Day
Could close the circuit of his annual Way
A quick Return, if Life indulg'd Desire
Should prove the Witness of your faithful Fire —
Give willing WALLIS to his OBRA's arms...
Thy faithful OBRA, aided by thy Hand,
Again shall rise, the Empress of the Land...

So now, she —

Asks, and entreats, in OBRA'S injur'd Name,
Thy wish'd-for Presence to restore her Fame,
Her haughty Foes, her Subjects' Fears remove,
And share at once her Empire and her love.

Cans't thou forget, how cheerful, how content
TAHEITEE'S Sons their Days of Pleasure spent:
With rising Morn they sought the healthful Stream,
And walk'd, or work'd till sultry Noon-tide came,
Then social join'd, from vain Distinctions free,
In Mirth convivial round the spreading Tree,
While tuneful Flutes, and warbling Wood-notes near,
In rival Strains still charm'd the list'ning Ear:
At grateful Eve they mix'd the artless Tale,
The Jest, the Dance, the vegetable Meal;
Paid the last Visit at some Fountain's Head,
To cleanse, and cool them for the peaceful Bed;
Deem'd the bright Sun declin'd for them alone,
These Isles the World, and all the World their own...

*Hence favour'd Man, with ev'ry Good supply'd,*
*Health in his Look, and Plenty at his Side,*
*His only Toil, Amidst the Forests free,*
*To point the Pearl-Hook, fell the stubborn Tree;*
*Or watch the swift Bonetas as they glide,*
*Launch the Canoe, and chace them with the Tide:*
*His manly Mirth too, on the Beach retir'd*
*Oft hast thou seen, and seeing still admired —*
*Lo! Now he mounts, as Surf-swollen Billows heave*
*Now sinks beneath, and wantons with the wave…*

*Ah! WALLIS haste, should yet that name remain*
*To crown my Hopes, and prove my Fears are vain!*
*Haste from the Land where Arts engender Strife,*
*And no an Art but rears some Foe to Life…*

*Yes, WALLIS, yes, from Thee no Fears alarm,*
*Whose highest Rage Submission could disarm —*
*Well do my Thoughts recall that awful Hour*
*When first we felt, and trembled at thy Pow'r*
*Some dreadful Demon, with an hostile Band,*
*We fear'd Thee sent to desolate our Land,*
*What could, alas! Defenceless Troops inspire?*
*What check the Fury of destructive Fire?*
*Repell'd, confounded, Patriot Valour fled,*
*As all  around the rapid Ruin sped,*
*Till first in Mercy, as the first in Sway,*
*Your Pity spar'd what Pow'r could take away,*
*Resistance conquer'd saw Resentment cease,*
*Hush'd was the Air, and rais'd each downcast Face;*

*'Twas then to meet Thee on the crowded Shore,*
*The peaceful Plantain in my Hand I bore,*
*In due Obeisance half my Bosom bar'd,*
*And fond Respect by mutual Rites rever'd …*

157

*Here, in thy fav'rite, fond TAHEITEE, still*
*It's sons obsequious, and it's Laws thy Will,*
*Thy faithful OBRA, aided by thy Hand,*
*Again shall rise, the Empress of the Land*
*Her Awe-struck Foes, to shun impending Ire,*
*Quick to the Mountains' silent Gloom retire;*
*Or prostrate — penitent — their Deeds deplore,*
*Her Wrongs redress, her Regal Rights restore;*
*Till, smiling Pace thro' ev'ry Region seen,*
*She rules triumphant, and expires — a Queen.*

It is impossible not to wonder how Samuel Wallis felt when he read this very popular ballad. There was every possibility that he would face public criticism for his treatment of his "Indian Queen," or so perhaps he feared. But, as it happened, he escaped all acrimony — because the world believed that he had written it himself!

The ballad-writer was in actual fact an Irishman, the Rev. Gerald Fitzgerald, but it was popularly thought that it had been composed by Captain Wallis, perhaps in self-recrimination, or perhaps as a plea to the authorities to make good the harm that the discovery had done to the Tahitians, by returning the island to a rural paradise. Until very recently, the catalogue of the British Library attributed it to him, and several modern reprints feature his name on the cover.

And, unlike the *Account of the Voyages*, it was very well received. Where Hawkesworth had portrayed Purea as lascivious, yet politically powerful, here she was a despondent outcast, greatly in need of a male, British, protector and defendant. It is noteworthy that while the dancers in the frontispiece of the ballad are bare-breasted, Purea is modestly clothed from neck to toe — as she is in the farewell scene that illustrated it.

As the *Critical Review* observed, the poet "rescued a subject from the hands of ridicule, which appears to have deserved a better fate."

*Wallis Memorial, Matavai Bay, Tahiti.*
Photo © Ron Druett 2017

# Chapter 15: Finale

By the year, 1779, when *The Injured Islanders* was published, Wallis had long left active naval service and was retired, with just the sinecure post of extra commissioner of the navy to make him feel busy. He led a quiet life, finally passing away on January 21, 1795, at his house in Portland Square, London. And the world did not even notice.

Forgotten long before he died, Wallis has been even more thoroughly forgotten since. Despite the rich legacy in art and literature that his voyage inspired, he has been lost to history. Incredibly, the top entry about him on the internet today opens with the sentence, "Little is known of Samuel Wallis," while yet another reflects, "He was apparently not a particularly keen explorer, and it was felt by many that he could have achieved far more during his voyage of discovery." Scholars write off Samuel Wallis as a captain who showed "little initiative", and make a point of the fact that - like all such discoveries - he found Tahiti by accident. His contemporaries were equally unkind.

Yet, the captain of the 1766 voyage of the *Dolphin* had so much to recommend him. It was the age of the lash and the press gang, where confused, ignorant men were scooped off the streets and beaten into subjection, and seamen could be hanged for trivial crimes, but Samuel Wallis, an unusually enlightened captain, treated his crews like a father.

Those men who arrived on board with nothing but dirty rags on their backs were supplied with clothes at his own expense, and though he disciplined when necessary, he was consistent and fair. His men openly revered him, writing a communal letter at the end of the voyage that thanked him for his "Humane and generous treatment." It is a testament to their loyalty that not a single one tried to leave him by jumping ship — something that is quite remarkable, when the allurement of the golden maidens of Tahiti is considered, and a record that James Cook could not match.

Wallis was also a fastidious housekeeper, insisting on a ship that was clean and well-aired. Typhus, a disease that was carried by body lice, and which flourished in damp, overcrowded, dirty, stuffy conditions, was so common on the berth decks of the time that it was known as "ship fever." Brought on board by men who had been living in the rookeries of the East End, or in jails, or on board other ships, the disease often took a dreadful toll even before the ship left home, killing so many that there were not enough left to weigh the anchor. Captains deplored the high death rate, but it was taken for granted that it was going to happen — life was cheap, back then, on land as well as sea.

Wallis had no typhus on board. The men did not have body lice, because he insisted on a dirt-free ship. He also made sure his seamen were as well-rested as possible, considering sleep necessary for good health. The usual shipboard routine was the two-watch system, where the seamen were divided into two teams alternating every four hours, which meant they slept in snatches. Instead, Captain Wallis had a three-watch arrangement, dividing his crew into three teams, so that on most sea-days every seaman was off-duty for a spell that lasted from six to eight hours, allowing for a decent sleep. In port, when the weather and repairs of the ship allowed it, he had a four-watch routine, where each man worked just eight hours a day.

With his surgeon, Dr John Hutchinson, Wallis counter-ed an epidemic of Java typhoid with such efficiency that the Admiralty gave Hutchinson's report to Cook, to carry around the world on the *Endeavour*. Dr Hutchinson noted that Captain Wallis sent his patients food from his own table, but Samuel Wallis was much more proactive than that — he converted the *Dolphin* into an infirmary that would have rivalled a seamen's hospital in England. The sick men were isolated from the rest, and the quarters were sanitised daily. As soon as a landfall was reached, a camp for the sick was set up on shore, where they were nursed until everyone had recovered. Remarkably, though forty men became gravely ill, only one died.

Wallis was also a pioneer in the prevention of scurvy, the horrifying disease of long voyages that was due to lack of vitamins in the diet. When the ship was in Madeira, he bought a large supply of lemons, and in the Straits of Magellan he sent men on shore to collect "sellery" or "scurvy grass" — as his surgeon, John Hutchinson, wrote, the sailors were given a "breakfast extraordinary", which was porridge boiled with the herbs they had foraged. In the Pacific, Wallis sent boat parties through the wild surf of far-flung atolls to trade for coconuts and harvest scurvy grass. When the ship was in Batavia, he took ten tons of limes on board. The highly unusual result was that when the *Dolphin* arrived home on May 20, 1768, after a voyage around the world lasting twenty-one months and nineteen days, not a single man had died of scurvy.

Wallis's ship-management was an example for all shipmasters, not just James Cook, and following his methods saved the lives of many thousands of future seamen. Yet, he missed out on the credit. He kept a little book in which he meticulously noted all 308 instances of sickness in his complement of 160 men, along with details of the six deaths (three from accidents, two from longstanding illness, and one from the typhoid epidemic), and this was sent to the Admiralty in October 1772, as stamped, notarized evidence of what he had achieved. Somehow, however, the Lords of the Admiralty found it easy to ignore.

And so it was James Cook who was hailed as the man who had carried his crews across the vast Pacific Ocean "without losing one man" from scurvy, and not the man who really deserved the accolade, Samuel Wallis.

The return of the *Dolphin* did not simply trigger a sudden rush of exploratory expeditions, but also changed the way people thought about the South Seas. No longer was the Pacific Ocean a daunting destination, reached by a tortuous, storm-ridden strait that was guarded at its mouth by giants, explored only because it was supposed by intellectuals that a great, unknown continent lurked somewhere in its expanse. It was now a beckoning sea, bejewelled by an island with spectacular vistas, a balmy climate, replete with exotic fruits ... and peopled by handsome young men, and gorgeous, doe-eyed, bare-breasted girls.

Where Europeans had been fixated with the idea of finding new continents in a hostile sea, tropical islands now became their dream. Life on Tahiti was described in idyllic terms by the first visitors, as a paradise where everyone was happy and no one had to work, the fertile soil producing everything a man could possibly want or need. It was a myth, of course — the soils of Tahiti and her sister islands produced only because of the devoted labour of skilled gardeners. But the pastoral paradise of the Pacific was (and is) a persistent and persuasive myth – and a seductive myth, too. As Wallis remarked, "The women are all handsome, and some of them extremely beautiful." It might have been an idealisation of the South Seas, but it was (and is) one that has inspired great painters and great writers, and one which led to the most famous mutiny in history, that of Bligh's *Bounty*.

Because that first discovery was so swiftly supplanted by the voyages of Captain James Cook, Europe forgot Samuel Wallis. The old Tahitians, by contrast, remembered him well, and recognized the sea-change in European perceptions of the Pacific that his discovery inspired. At Point Venus, on Matavai Bay, the memorial for Cook is a small, vaguely phallic ball atop a post, enclosed in a low railing, while the monument to the captain of the *Dolphin*, Samuel Wallis, is a towering lighthouse-like structure.

The men who dedicated it to him knew that the visit of the *Dolphin* was a pivotal moment in the story of not just the island, but of the entire south Pacific. The tales Wallis and his sailors told brought fame, legend, and visitors to their island. And still it is so today.

*The great writers, Conrad, Maugham and Melville, spent only a few years in the South Seas, but their memory of those waters was indestructible; for the nature of life in the islands commands attention to the vivid world and its even more vivid inhabitants.*

- James Michener

*Consider the subtleness of the sea; how its most dreaded creatures glide under water, unapparent for the most part, and treacherously hidden beneath the loveliest tints of azure. Consider also the devilish brilliance and beauty of many of its most remorseless tribes, as the dainty embellished shape of many species of sharks. Consider, once more, the universal cannibalism of the sea; all whose creatures prey upon each other, carrying on eternal war since the world began.*

*Consider all this; and then turn to the green, gentle, and most docile earth; consider them both, the sea and the land; and do you not find a strange analogy to something in yourself? For as this appalling ocean surrounds the verdant land, so in the soul of man there lies one insular Tahiti, full of peace and joy, but encompassed by all the horrors of the half-known life. God keep thee! Push not off from that isle, thou canst never return!"*

- Herman Melville

*Tahiti is very far away, and I knew that I should never see it again. A chapter of my life was closed, and I felt a little nearer to inevitable death.*

— Somerset Maughan

*She rolls a Tahitian cigarette and stretches out on the bed to smoke. Her feet with a mechanical gesture continually caress the wood of the foot-end. Her expression becomes gentler, it visibly softens, her eyes shine, and a regular hissing sound escapes from her lips. I imagine that I am listening to a purring cat that is meditating on some bloody sensuality.*

*As I am changeable, I find her now very beautiful, and when she said to me with a throbbing voice, "You are nice," a great trouble fell upon me. Truly the princess was delicious…*

*Doubtless in order to please me, she began to recite a fable, one of La Fontaine's, The Cricket and the Ants - a memory of her childhood days with the sisters who had taught her…*

*"Do you know, Gauguin," said the princess in rising, "I do not like your La Fontaine."*

*"What? Our good La Fontaine?"*

*"Perhaps, he is good, but his morals are ugly. The ants..." (and her mouth expressed disgust) "Ah, the crickets, yes. To sing, to sing, always to sing!"*

*And proudly without looking at me, the shining eyes fixed upon the far distance, she added, "How beautiful our realm was when nothing was sold there! All the year through the people sang ... To sing always, always to give!"*

*And she left.*

*I put my head back on the pillow, and for a long time I was caressed by the memory of the syllables:*

*"Ia orana, Gauguin."*

– Paul Gauguin, *Noa Noa*

# ROGERS RICHARDSON'S POETICAL ESSAY OF THE VOYAGE

The ship's barber, Rogers Richardson, composed a "poetical essay" on the homeward leg of the voyage, and presented it to Wallis, who copied it into his logbook.

## THE
## *DOLPHIN'S JOURNAL*
### *Epitomiz'd in a poetical Essay.*

*Let Holland, France, or haughty Spain*
*Boast their Discoveries o'er the Main,*
*And sing their Hero's mighty Fame,*
*Which now with Time decays.*
*Britannia's Isle, at length has found*
*A Man who sail'd the Globe all round*
*Discovering Isles, till now unfound,*
*And well deserves the Bays.*

*WALLIS I sing, the Hero brave,*
*Who to his Country, like a Slave*
*Undaunted plow'd the Southern Wave,*
*In search of Land unfound.*
*His Ship the Dolphin, and his Crew,*

*All young, and hearty, tho' but few,*
*Yet with him dauntless, bold, and true,*
*They sail'd the Globe all round.*

*A welcome Breeze fills every sail,*
*No more the Maiden's Tears avail,*
*For Honour o'er their Tears prevail.*
*Adieu to Plymouth Sound.*
*Ye Virgins fair, forbear to weep,*
*For you sincere our Hearts we'll keep,*
*For you we'll Plough th'extensive Deep,*
*And sail the Globe all round.*

*Madeira first supply'd our Need,*
*St. Jago next, from thence with Speed,*
*Whilst Oxen for us daily bleed,*
*To West our Course we steer.*
*The well known Straights, we enter than,*
*So fam'd for it's Gigantick Men,*
*Whose height from six Feet reach'd to ten,*
*And safely anchor there.*

*As farther thro' the Streights we go,*
*Where lofty Clifts are tipp'd with Snow,*
*And rapid Cataracts swiftly flow,*
*All down their craggy Sides.*
*Where Winter too, incessant reigns,*
*And Aeolus, might God disdains*
*To curb the Winds, who free from Chains,*
*Our Art almost derides.*

*Some Natives here, tho' few we find*
*A Savage Race of Human Kind,*
*Scarce blest with Sense, to reason blind,*
*In Ignorance rudely bred.*

*Nought to defend their swarthy Sides,*
*But beasts or Fishes nauseous Hides,*
*More nauseous Food, and nought besides,*
*Mossy Ground their Bed.*
*Into the wide pacific Seas,*
*From such unpleasing sights as these,*
*Waft us some fair auspicious Breeze,*
*And be our constant Guard.*
*The might God, the Pray'r receiv'd*
*Our Sails we loose, our Ship reliev'd,*
*The Streights we clear, and undeceiv'd,*
*Our Toils he well rewards.*

*No longer now our Griefs he mocks.*
*No more in Streights, our Ship he locks,*
*From Dangers freed we see those Rocks,*
*A Distance far behind.*
*Pleas'd with the Change those Dangers o'er,*
*With Joy we view the distant Shore,*
*And bless the God, whose awful Pow'r*
*Is ever inconfin'd.*

*Now fraught with Wind, our Canvas swell,*
*Tho' some rude Squalls our Ship assail,*
*Yet all in vain, they naught avail,*
*Wide from the dang'rous Coast.*
*For Neptune kind, with pleasant Gales,*
*For some few Weeks, repleats our Sails,*
*And on his Son such Fame entails,*
*As Europe ne'er could boats.*

*Swiftly he wafts us o'er the Waves,*
*Grants ev'ry Boon our Hero craves,*
*Scarce in the Southern Sea he leaves*
*An Isle to him unshown.*

*Respecting every Son of Fame,*
*Great Wallis gives to each a Name,*
*With Titles free, froother's Claim,*
*But trusts to Fate his own.*
*On Whitsunday the first was seen*
*Which bore that name – with*
*The next to Britain's royal queen*
*Charlotte's name was fixt*
*Some few we pass, in number four*
*Whose names are still reserved in stone*
*The next the royal bishop's bore*
*And George, great George, the next.*

*Here wait, my muse, a while to view*
*A beauteous scene, to Britons new*
*Whose climate equall'd is by few*
*The British Monarch's isle*
*And O! My muse, thou heavenly maid*
*An artless bard invokes thy aid*
*Let all his skill be here display'd*
*And on his efforts smile.*

*The anchors well secur'd in ground*
*Sails furl'd, yards, top-masts lower'd*
*Well pleas'd, we view the fertile ground*
*Well worth a Monarch's care*
*Safe in Port-Royal bay we ride*
*Where no rude wind, nor rapid tide*
*Or rugged rocks, unseen abide*
*But all's serene and fair.*

*The dauntless Indians round us flock*
*With each a pittance from his stock*
*Which they for various trifles truck*
*Content with what we spare*

171

Off on our ship, they fix their eye
As oft on us, with deep surprise
And deem our floating world a prize
For them next morn to share.
Prepar'd next morn with stones they came
Which well they hurl'd with dextrous aim
But soon were all repuls'd with flame
And some canoes unmann'd
Fatal attempt, ambitious thought
Poor simple men, too late you're taught
That Britons ne'er are easy caught
With schemes badly plann'd.

No safe retreat they now can find
For dire destruction unconfin'd
Our balls swift whistling through the wind
O'ertakes the insulting hand
But oh! To paint their vast surprise
The terror sparkling in their eyes
Or their confus'd and hideous cries
Requires an abler hand.

Then cease, my Muse, the canoes' war
Is ceas'd; the Vanquish'd make for peace
Their comrades fate with tears deplore
And seek a speedy flight.
A gentler theme demands your care
To paint the beauteous life prepare
Whilst we fatigu'd, tho' void of fear
In slumbers pass the night.

The morning dawns, the well-known call
From gentle sleep awakens us all,
The boats well mann'd and arm'd withal
The conquer'd isle we claim

*Down at the sea-beach side we make*
*The islanders their huts forsake*
*And we in form possession take*
*In George's royal name*
*Now free to range, we find rich fruits*
*Pits, fowls, and most salubrious roots*
*Refreshments, such as aptly suits*
*The seaman's briny food.*
*For all of these, an iron bar*
*Or sixty nails, more precious far*
*To them. Ev'n gold or diamonds are*
*Less valu'd, less approv'd.*

*The natives polish'd, better far*
*Than other  savage Indians are*
*The girls well featur'd, passing fair,*
*And kind to us in all respects.*
*The men well made, robust and tall,*
*Subject to none, by some enthrall'd*
*Thoughtless of ev'ry future call*
*The live as sense directs.*

*In tillage quite an artless hand,*
*But Nature kindly tills their land*
*Whose fertile soil, at her command*
*Yields all the sweet of life.*
*At least such necessary store*
*That pleas'd with that, they seek no more*
*Nor covet gold, or silver ore*
*The common source of strife.*

*The slender garb, their bodies hide*
*Is far too curious to describe*
*Invention here has well supply'd*
*With nicest art their wants*

173

Friend, ye artist of the trade
Whom here I seek not to degrade
It's neither spun nor wove, but made
From wild and simple plants.
Light as our English ladies' sacks
But made of neither silk nor flax,
Cotton, nor wool, tho' white as wax,
And wrought with matchless pains;
Some coarse, some fine, some painted o'er,
Some plain, in breadth three yards or more,
And oft in length some seven score,
Each curious piece contains.

A purling stream thro' ev'ry grove,
As crystal clear, as seen to rove,
Whose flowery banks, tho' none improve,
Unnumber'd vales adorn,
Whilst unmolest'd, birds unite,
To form the rural sweet delight
Calling with various notes each night,
And offering in the morn.

A thousand beauties, more's too few,
To give this royal isle its due
But here I cease, lest these, tho' true,
Should form romantic talk:
Yet let me not in silence pass'
What well in this deserves a place
An island sacred to his Grace
The Royal Duke of York.

Which here in view in grandeur rears,
Proud of the royal name it bears,
High as the lofty glitt'ring stars,
Its ever-verdant head;

174

Beneath whose shades a pleasant bourne,
Which various fragrant shrubs adorn
And beauteous flowers daily borne
Around its borders spread.

But hark! The Boatswain's call how shrill!
Up anchors, boys, your topsails fill
And staysails hoist, with free good will
Each jovial tar obeys,
And now we dare the waves once more
Ne'er plowed by Europe's keels before,
Discov'ring still a long-hid shore
Of isles within these seas.

For daily now fresh land we make
And all in course their titles take
Saunders and How the first partake,
Next Scylla's isle we spy.
A beauteous island next we made,
Be that Boscawen's Wallis said,
Tho' low in dust the hero's laid,
His name shall never die.

The next we made was Keppel's isle,
Where nature kindly seem'd to smile,
Fertile in fruits, as rich in soil,
Inferior to none.

Then several days with gentle gales,
Smooth seas, nor more than half-fill'd sails,
Elaps'd, but Neptune scorn'd to fail
A work so well begun.

Pleas'd with his noble gen'rous soul
Who rather chose the same t'enroll

175

*Of absent friends, than keep the whole,*
*T'immortalise his own.*
*An island that the god prepar'd,*
*Which just at dawn of day appear'd,*
*And thus the friendly monarch's heard,*
*T'address his darling son.*

*Wallis, be this your own! He said,*
*Rearing above the waves his head.*
*Whilst Nereids round the godhead spread,*
*And all approve the fame.*
*From me your sire, my son, receive,*
*With laurels such as I shall give*
*This isle, which time shall ne'er outlive,*
*But ever crown your fame.*

*Pursue your voyage with utmost speed,*
*May ev'ry future wish succeed,*
*Long may you wear what fate's decreed,*
*Should only crown your brow.*
*Myself will o'er the dang'rous seas*
*Escort you safe where-e'er you please,*
*Then disappear'd. A gentle breeze,*
*Confirm'd the sov'reign's vow. ...*

*Homeward our Voyage we now pursue,*
*But long before the Cape's in view,*
*A dreadful Flux, seiz'd half our Crew,*
*And ghastly Death appear'd.*
*Yet scarce th'Almighty'Aid implor'd,*
*E'er Heav'n all kind, our Health restor'd,*
*And only two of all on Board,*
*The dire Effects has shar'd.*
*Now O my Muse, aloud proclaim,*
*Once more our much lov'd Captain's Name,*

*Nor leave exempt from circling Fame,*
*One Officer apart.*
*To Heav'n, and them, our Loves we owe,*
*As fuller Journals best can shew,*
*By them their daily Care you'll know,*
*Unmix'd with flattering Art ...*

*Be kind, ye Gales, and waft us o'er,*
*These briney Waves to Britain's Shoar,*
*Let us with Joy, behold once more,*
*Our much lov'd native Land.*
*Then shall this Voyage in Lists of Fame,*
*Immortalize the Dolphin's Name,*
*Wrote in a more aspiring Strain*
*By some more able Hand....*

# Commentary

## 1. *Journals and logbooks of the* Dolphin *voyage, 1766-68*

Logbooks and shipboard journals come in set forms. The deck-log was a formal affair, each page ruled up for hourly notations of wind, weather, course sailed, and the position of the ship, plus remarkable events such as punishments, sickness, accidents, or death. Usually there was a note of food served out to the crew, partly to stave off future complaints. In port, work done on board and provisions procured on shore were also recorded.

The log might be kept by one man, or the hourly notation might be made by whoever was "on watch" (was in charge of the deck at the time — officers, just like seamen, stood watches.) The sea-day started at noon and ended at noon, when the date changed, becoming twelve hours ahead of the civil day, though the logbook keeper might correct this when the ship was in port. This can lead to some confusion about the precise dates of events, as one logbook keeper would keep to ship time while at Tahiti, while another changed to civil time. This is particularly obvious when comparing the logs kept by George Robertson and Captain Wallis.

Shipboard journals (occasionally, confusingly, called "logbooks" by their owners), were more like diaries, as interesting events were described in detail, and the lines dividing up the page could be ignored. A journal where the account was written on the same day, or soon afterward, can be very useful indeed, especially if the writer has added personal comments and observations. The longer the delay between the event and its recording, the more likely the journal has become colored by vagaries of memory, the illumination of hindsight, or conversations with shipmates. The researcher has to make constant value judgments.

A basic source was the daily logbook kept by Captain Samuel Wallis, a scrawled, spontaneous account now held at the Mitchell Library, New South Wales, Australia (J27951). Wallis created a revised journal by transposing, adapting, and lengthening logbook entries. This was a "public" journal, destined for publication. It is now held at the Public Record Office (PRO) London (Adm 55/35), with penciled notes by Hawkesworth in the margins.

Before Wallis handed it over, a copy was made, evidently for his own use; this is now at the Alexander Turnbull Library in Wellington, New Zealand, (qMS-2114), and is interesting because of additions in Wallis's script, including a list of artifacts handed over to the Admiralty. Otherwise it is identical to the public journal.

That there are two Wallis accounts — the rough logbook and the revised journal — presented problems, as the differences between them are striking, particularly in Tahiti. Wallis was very ill when he wrote the logbook (meaning a lot could be missing), while his public journal was written to put his actions in the best light possible (meaning it may not be dependable). For instance, it is likely he magnified his association with "the Queen," to add legitimacy to his "possession" of Tahiti.

Accounts written by the sailing master, George Robertson, vary too. The most important collection is held at the PRO as Adm 51/4539. This includes an informal diary, written on the spot. There is also a revision of this,

179

probably in imitation of Wallis. A lot of subjective material is added to this public journal (including sexual adventures coyly described as happening to "my friend"), along with retrospective comments that make it evident it was written after arrival in London.

Robertson was a vivid writer, and it is a racy and fascinating read. Though never mentioned as a source, it was used by Hawkesworth, as there are penciled notations in the same hand as those in the Wallis public journal. It was eventually (1948) edited by Hugh Carrington, and published by the Hakluyt Society. A modernized version appeared later, edited by Warner. Where I used the published version, I chose Carrington (1948), being more accurate.

To complicate matters still further, there are more Robertson versions. Another box, Adm 51/4540, holds his very interesting journal on HMS *Swift*, beginning March 1, 1763, ending 29 May 1766, and encompassing the wreck of the ship, followed by a neat transcription of the *Dolphin* diary. Some sentences are corrected, and there is the occasional added detail, but on the whole they are the same. Another Robertson account is a long appendix to Wallis's public journal (the one with annotations by Hawkesworth). After ending on May 19, 1768, and signing it "Saml Wallis," the captain added several pages of navigational observations. Then Robertson took over the book to write descriptions of landfalls, including a seven-page description of Tahiti, basically an abstract of his journal, but with additional material. It is signed "George Robertson."

Also at the PRO are logs and journals kept by other men. Adm 51/4538 includes two deck-logs, one entirely in the hand of William Clarke, first lieutenant, and the other in various scripts (including Robertson's). There is also a journal by Clarke, but apart from a few longer entries at Tahiti, it is as brief as the deck-logs, probably because of his ill health. Others, kept by Francis Wilkinson, William Luke, Humphrey West, "Mr Douglas Carpenter," and Benjamin Butler, are boxed together as Adm 51/4541; and those by George Pinnock, Henry Ibbott, Tobias Furneaux, and Hambly are collected as Adm 51/4542.

Pinnock's begins on "July ye 16th 1766 at Deptford," and ends at Tinian, where he writes "Finis." Ibbott's begins 15 July 1766, and ends 10 December 1767 at Batavia. It includes a long description of Tahiti and the people, which must have been written over several days, because it is dated 4 July but includes things he learned later, such as the method of making tapa.

Lieutenant Furneaux's log is made up of technical entries, while Hambly's is very brief, with the occasional blank page, as if he meant to write more when he got around to it. Box Adm. 51/4543 has equally uninformative logs kept by Francis Pender, Samuel Horsenail, and Thomas Coles (though Pender has rousing descriptions of the battles). Adm 51/4544 has a journal kept by John Nichols, and two more by George Pinnock and Humphrey West, with very similar entries to their previous records.

There is also a journal kept by John Gore. When Wallis collected the logs, Gore flatly refused to hand his over. "Mr Gore Mate of this Ship was the only person that took any umbrage at it," wrote Wallis in his logbook. Evidently, he gave in and let Gore keep it, as the journal is now held at the National Library of Australia, Canberra (MS 4), and is not part of the Admiralty holdings. I am grateful to the librarians who interloaned a microfilm to me. It is hard to tell why Gore made a fuss, as it contains no indiscretions. It ends 16 October 1767, leaving Tinian, and is signed "Jno Gore, Master Hunter."

## 2: *The Arrival at Tahiti*:

"We are now in the Greatest hopes of Seeing the Southern Continent," wrote Robertson on first sighting (19 June 1767, Adm 51/4540). In his addendum to Wallis's public journal (Adm 55/35) he wrote "all the full Grown Men and Women Paint there Arms, Legs, and thighs, with a Black sort of Stuff."

His story of the men grunting like hogs etc. is in his public journal and does not appear in the earlier records. Wallis, in his logbook, simply says that they showed the shipboard animals to the natives. Wilkinson, however, notes June 20 that they imitated the sounds. The story of the goat scaring the islander appears only in Wallis's public journal.

The order of events as the ship skirted the coast is taken from Wallis's logbook, with additions from Robertson's public journal. Wallis provided details of the conflict in Matavai Bay omitted by Robertson, so his account is the basis of this story. The feather amulet — '*ura-tatae* — is described by Oliver (1974): 75-6, and Henry, 13. Also see Ferdon, 64.

John Nicholls described seeing "Quantities of stones" in the canoes, and was another to describe the shot woman (24 July 1767). While the mention of conch-shell trumpets might seem anachronistic, as the usual belief is they were introduced to Tahiti after European arrival, Wallis's list of Tahitian artifacts delivered to the Admiralty included a "Conque."

The identity of the chief or priest who led the assault is unknown. Thomson (35-36) offers the possibility it was Amo, also strongly implied by Wilson (1799): x. Thomson describes Amo watching the ship from concealment on the hill (a crucial word is missed out, so it might have been a rock, though more likely a tree), which indicates he was afraid of being recognized by the Europeans. That he survived is another factor: while it would be easy for the Tahitians to name a dead man as the misguided priest or ill-advised chief who led the attack, it was not diplomatic to point the finger at someone who was still alive. No living chief (or high priest) would confess to taking a leading part in the debacle.

Wilkinson described the marines going "through their excises with the gratest regularity, the Indians facing of them within pistol shott of them after which the Lieutent advanced with an English pendent and took possession of the isl<sup>d.</sup>"

For the events that followed, I used all accounts written by Robertson and Wallis, plus Hawkesworth, 271-73. Details vary: Wallis said the old man came to the ship on his own, while Robertson says he came with a friend.

While in his public journal Robertson says the pennant was removed by the Tahitians right away, his logbook says they "carried it off at night." The alleged attack on the watering party is based on Wallis's logbook, with added details from Furneaux, Nicholls, and Robertson. All shipboard accounts tell the same basic story, that the Europeans were facing another attempt to seize the ship.

For the significance of the presentation of tapa, see Serge Tcherkézoff's chapter, "On Cloth, Gifts and Nudity: Regarding Some European Misunderstandings During Early Encounters in Polynesia," in Colchester, pp. 51-58; for the manufacture of tapa, see Ferdon, pp. 111-117.

Robertson described the trading procedure and the restriction on crossing the river in his revised journal (Robertson 1948, 168-70). The quotes come from Wallis's logbook, 29-30 June 1767. Robertson's story of the "Dear Irish boy" is in his public journal, 6 July 1767; there is no such mention in his logbook.

Scarr (73) notes islanders found Europeans foul-smelling. Spaarman (69) commented islanders were fascinated by white skin. Quotes from Ibbott are taken from a discursive page dated 4 July, obviously expanded later. Wallis first noted prying off cleats for the nails in his public journal, 11 July 1767.

Adams (50) recorded Purea taking over the *fare hau*. Henry points out (15) Purea was advised and seconded in all her actions by Tupaia; there is nothing in the *Endeavour* accounts, or records kept on Cook's later voyages, to indicate she was naturally so resourceful.

Wallis noted the method of buying trees for firewood in his logbook 9 July, the same day he described Jonathan's first visit, but did not mention either in his revised journal. Robertson mentioned the wood-cutting in his revised journal on the same date (Robertson 1948, 183), but delayed describing Purea's interference and Jonathan's visit until the following day's entry, when he devoted a great deal of detail to both (Robertson 1948, 186-89). His logbook and addendum to Wallis's revised journal note the same events, much more briefly, on the same dates.

Confusingly, Wilkinson's description of seeing the "large house" and the visit of the "Queen" on board "with some of her Attendance" are both dated 16 July, so must be retrospective. The christening of "Jonathan" appears only in Robertson's public journal (Robertson 1948: 188-89). Wallis noted, "This man we called Jonathan," in his rough log, but did not mention it in his revised journal, which is probably why it does not appear in Hawkesworth.

In his addendum to Wallis's revised journal, Robertson notes briefly on 14 July, "This Day the Queen came off to see the Ship for the first time," but does not mention it in any of his own logs. Consequently, the description of her experiences on board comes from Wallis's logbook and journal, which are both dated 13 July, and tell the same basic story.

The difference between his dating and Robertson's is easily accounted for by the 12-hour difference between sea-time and shore-time. Years afterward (1785), the *Dolphins*' colorful descriptions of their queen provided the inspiration for a theatrical costume for a pantomime, "Omai, or a Trip Around the World." The character of Purea, "Obereyan Enchantress," was sketched by de Loutherbourg, designer of the pantomime, who also sketched the Tahitian (actually Raiatean) dancer.

That Wallis went to "the Queen's House" the morning after her first visit occurred *only* in his revised journal. In his logbook, the entire entry following her visit to the ship reads: "AM the weather so bad could send no Boat onshoar, the Natives came down to the Watering Place and Cut the Bank of the River and made a New Channell, as the water has Risen very much on the flat ground—this forenoon came of two Chiefs & brought with them some Roasted Pigs & fruit, gave them presents in return." His visit is not described in his logbook until 22 July 1767, and then in almost the same words as those in the public journal for 13/14 July.

The difference is puzzling. There is a good chance that 22 July is correct, and Wallis brought the date of his visit forward when he revised his journal, knowing that delaying such an important event would not look good on his record. None of the other journal-keepers mention the visit to the *fare hau* — not even Clarke, who was supposed to be there — so there is no confirmation of either date. Because Hawkesworth made the 13 July date standard, it is the one I have used.

Wallis's beautiful scale drawing, "A Ground plan, & Eliva-tion of the Queens House at King Georges Island, in the South Seas, taken in July 1767," is held with his logbook at the Mitchell Library, Sydney. The anecdote about the surgeon removing his wig is given in Hawkesworth (291), and must have stemmed from a personal communication, as it is not mentioned in any of the records.

Wallis's logbook entry for 18 July 1767 reads, "this day the Queen shewed herself again she having been absent some days," while his revised journal merely mentions she came to the beach. Robertson described entertaining the Tahitian nobles in the gunroom in his logbook entry for 18 July. In his revised journal a much more detailed recounting is dated 19 July for the morning events (the feast at the *fare hau*) and 20 July for the afternoon events (Purea's visit on board).

It is also here that Pickersgill is named as Gallagher's companion on the stroll. This is the first mention of "the Queen" in any of Robertson's own records, save a 14 July notation in his addendum to Wallis's journal, where he describes her attendants being dressed in white. The story of the breakfast, Robertson's visit to the *fare hau*, and his flirtation with Purea comes entirely from Robertson's revised journal.

For the *tapu* nature of the head, see Steiner, 45-46. *Tabu*, which the English adopted as "taboo," is a Tongan word; the Tahitian word, like the Maori, is *tapu*. Adams (51) details the disastrous implications for Amo, Purea, and Tupaia of Wallis's failure to visit Papara.

For a discussion of John Harrison's method of finding longitude by using a pre-publication copy of Maskelyne's tables, see Richardson, 29.

Robertson's angry tirade about his shipmates' suspicions of Purea's "Treacherous designe" is in his addendum to Wallis's revised journal. Wilkinson's comment about "the Indians suspecting we Ware going away" is dated 26 July 1767; in the same entry he described weighing the sheet anchor and setting up the topgallant masts and yards. The stream anchor had been weighed on 24 July. Pinnock's entry about the gunner was dated 26 July.

Wallis's journal states that the queen came on board while the ship was getting underway, but in his logbook he is definite that she did not: "the Queen kept in her Canoe at the gunroom Port, & wept very much." None of the other logbooks or journals mention her boarding the ship at this time, so it seems likely Wallis's memory was faulty.

Robertson noted they dressed two chiefs "in the European manner" (13 July 1767) in all accounts, but named Jonathan as one of the chiefs in only his revised journal. (Robertson 1948: 193.)


## 3: Dolphin's *arrival home*

Wallis made the decision to abandon the hunt for the phantom continent on 15 August 1767, indicating in his revised journal that he had accomplished enough by discovering a good source of "the refreshments that may be had for any future expedition," and that it was "most prudent and more for the benefit of His Maj's Service to make the best of my way to Tinian, Batavia & to Europe."

187

His account of the "inhabitants of Otaheite" is in rough draft in his logbook, while the version that was submitted to the Admiralty can be read on the National Library of Australia website, "Voyages in the Southern Hemisphere."

Wallis's logbook provides a fascinating day-to-day account of the medical and dietary care of his men. Wine was considered better than grog, which was spirit (brandy in the *Dolphins'* case) mixed with water, because wine was acid, and acid was supposed to prevent and cure scurvy. (Wine is acid because of its tartaric acid content, and has no vitamin C, but Wallis was acting by the best principles he knew.) An interesting exposition on the preparation and medical uses of "Salep" or saloup was published in *Scots Magazine*, vol. XXX (1768, but dated Oct. 29, 1767): 8. Hutchinson's letter, dated May 16, 1768, is included with the first volume of the *Endeavour* log held at National Library of Australia, Canberra (MS 1)

Papers running the sensational story (after *Lloyd's*) were *The St. James's Chronicle* (May 24-26), *The London Chronicle* (May 24-26), and *The Gazetteer and New Daily Advertiser* (May 26-27). It was still running as late as July: *Scots Magazine*, vol. XXX, July 1768, pp. 378-79. This is the one quoted, though all the stories were exactly the same. Williams's paper "The *Endeavour* Voyage: A coincidence of motives" (2005: 3-18) is an excellent recounting of events after the *Dolphin* arrived home.

For contemporary documentation of the sailors' strike, see *Scots Magazine*, vol. XXX, June 1768, 328-30. The *Dolphin* was most probably laid up ("mothballed," in modern terminology) because the next muster for her was not until April 1770, and she was broken up soon after that. The dismissal of their petition was printed in the same magazine on p. 379.

The pay rates of the men, and the fate of Robertson are described by Carrington (Robertson 1948): xxxviii-xlii. Careers of Furneaux, Molyneux, Pickersgill, and Gore are summarized in Robson 2004: 105, 106-07, 151, 178. Francis Wilkinson, who went on to write a beautifully penned log of the voyage of the *Endeavour*, is a shadowy, undocumented figure, apart from the brief notation on the muster roll that he was born in Chatham in 1747.

William Perry, the assistant surgeon of the *Endeavour* reminisced about the voyage in a series of posts to the *Gentleman's Magazine*. His story about the seamen making sure they were "rich in iron" before leaving for Tahiti was published in the issue for July 1808, page 598.

The ballad "The Injured Islanders" can be read freely online as a google book. Rogers Richardson's "poetical ballad" is interesting because it is the only documentary evidence that Moorea ("Duke of York Island") was visited by the *Dolphin*s during the time in Tahiti. It is also a confirmation of the reverence of the crew for their captain.

# Bibliography

Adams, Henry. *Tahiti*. (Edited by Robert E. Spiller.)
Memoirs of Arii Taimai, the last chiefess of Papara
(and Purea's great-niece), as told to Adams through
Marau Taaroa, "last queen of Tahiti", who
translated. Paris: privately printed, 1901.

Ballantyne, Tony (editor). *Science, Empire and the
European Exploration of the Pacific*. London: Pacific
World Series (Ashgate), 2004.

Colchester, Chloe. *Clothing the Pacific*. UK: Berg, 2003.

Crawford, Peter. *Nomads of the Wind, A Natural History
of Polynesia*. London: BBC books, 1993.

De Bovis, Edmond. *Tahitian Society Before the Arrival of
the Europeans*. (Translated & edited by Robert D.
Craig.) Honolulu: Institute for Polynesian Studies,
Brigham Young University, 1976.

Dunmore, John. *Storms and Dreams: Louis de
Bougainville, Soldier, Explorer, Statesman*. Auckland:
Exisle, 2005.

Dunmore, John. *French Explorers in the Pacific*. 2 vv.
Oxford University Press, 1965-69.

Edwards, Philip. *Story of the Voyage, sea-narratives in
Eighteenth Century England*. Cambridge University
Press, 1994.

Ellis, William. *Polynesian Researches…* London: G. Robinson, 1782. The image of the ceremonial canoe came from this.

Ferdon, Edwin N. *Early Tahiti, As the Explorers Saw It, 1767-1797.* University of Arizona Press, 1981.

Finney, Ben R. *Polynesian Peasants and Proletarians.* Cambridge, Ma.: Schenkman Publishing, 1973.

Frost, Alan, with Jane Samson (editors). *Pacific Empires: essays in honour of Glyndwr Williams.* University of British Columbia, 1999.

Furneaux, Rupert. *Tobias Furneaux, Circumnavigator.* London: Cassell, 1960.

Hawkesworth, John. *An Account of the Voyages Undertaken by the Order of His Present Majesty … by Commodore Byron, Captain Wallis, Captain Carteret and Captain Cook, in the Dolphin, the Swallow, and the Endeavour …* London: Strahan and Cadell, 1773.

Henry, Teuira. *Ancient Tahiti.* Honolulu: Bernice Bishop Museum Bulletin 48, 1928.

Howarth, David. *Tahiti, a Paradise Lost.* London: Horvill, 1983.

Lincoln, Margarette (editor). *Science and Exploration in the Pacific: European Voyages to the Southern Oceans in the 18th Century.* London: Boydell with National Maritime Museum, 1998.

Lummis, Trevor. *Pacific Paradises, the Discovery of Tahiti & Hawaii.* London: Sutton, 2005.

Nussbaum, Felicity A. (editor). *The Global Eighteenth Century.* Baltimore: John Hopkins University Press, 2003.

Oliver, Douglas L. *Ancient Tahitian Society.* (3 vv.) Australian National University Press and University of Hawaii Press, 1974.

Richardson, Brian W. *Longitude and Empire: How Captain Cook's Voyages Changed the World.* University of British Columbia Press, 2005.

Robertson, George. *Discovery of Tahiti ... written by her master George Robertson.* Edited by Hugh Carrington. London: Hakluyt Society, 1948 (second series, No. XCVIII).

Robertson, George. *Account of the discovery of Tahiti ...* Edited by Oliver Warner. London: Folio Press, 1955.

Rodger, N.A.M. *The Wooden World, an Anatomy of the Georgian Navy.* London: HarperCollins, 1986.

Robson, John. *The Captain Cook Encyclopaedia.* Auckland: Random House, 2004.

Rogers, Shef. "Composing Conscience: the 'Injur'd Islanders' (1799) and English Sensibility," in, *The Eighteenth Century*, v. 38. No. 3, Fall, 1997.

Scarr, Deryck. *A History of the Pacific Islands: Passages Through Tropical Time.* New York: Routledge, 2000.

Smith, Bernard. *Imagining the Pacific in the wake of the Cook voyages.* Melbourne: Miegunyah Press, 1992.

Sparrman, Anders. *A Voyage Round the World with Captain James Cook in HMS* Resolution. London: Robert Hale, 1944.

Steiner, Franz Baermann. *Taboo.* London: Cohen & West, 1956. This valuable study has been reprinted as, *Taboo, Truth, and Religion,* in volume 1 of the *Selected Writings* of Franz Baermann Steiner series. (Edited by Jeremy Adler and Richard Fardon.) New York: Berghahn Books, 1999.

Thomas, Nicholas. *In Oceania: Visions, Artifacts, Histories.* London: Durham, 1997.

Thomson, Rev. R. Manuscript called "History of Tahiti" (London Missionary Society archives, Mitchell Library, Sydney, ms 660).

Truss, Lynne. "A bad book review can kill you — look at the case of John Hawkesworth. *The Guardian*, January 13, 2017.

Williams, Glyndwr. *Buccaneers, Explorers and Settlers: British Enterprises and Encounters in the Pacific 1670-1800*. London: Variorium Collected Studies (Ashgate), 2005.

Williams, Glyndwr, with Alan Frost. *Terra Australis to Australia*, Oxford University Press, 1989.

Wilson, James. *A Missionary Voyage to the Southern Pacific Ocean, Performed … in the ship* Duff. London: T. Chapman, 1799.

Wilson, Timothy. *Flags at Sea*. London: National Maritime Museum, 1986.

Old Salt Press is an independent press catering to those who love good books about ships and the sea. We are an association of writers working together to produce the very best of nautical and maritime fiction and non-fiction. We invite you to join us as we go down to the sea in books.

# From other Old Salt Press authors

## Honour Bound
— In this, the tenth book of the Fighting Sail series, Commander King is seized by the enemy. In an atmosphere of mounting tension, he is forced to survive in hostile territory.

## The Blackstrap Station
— Christmas 1803, and there is nothing to celebrate, as the shipwrecked crew of HMS *Prometheus* are forced to pit their wits against the enemy force sent out to hunt them down.

## HMS *Prometheus*
— In the eighth book of the Fighting Sail series, HMS *Prometheus* sets sail from the shipyard at Gibraltar, to face the greatest challenge yet.

## The Scent of Corruption

— Sir Richard Banks is appointed to HMS *Prometheus*, a seventy-four gun line-of-battleship which an eager Admiralty loses no time in ordering to sea — a non-stop nautical thriller in the best traditions of the genre.

## The Torrid Zone
— She's a tired ship with a worn out crew, but *HMS Scylla* has one more trip to make before her much postponed re-fit — a trip fraught with unexpected dangers.

## The Guinea Boat

— Set in Hastings, Sussex during the early part of 1803, *Guinea Boat* tells the story of two young lads, and the diverse paths they take to make a living on the water.

## Turn a Blind Eye

— Autumn, 1801. Newly appointed to the local revenue cutter, Commander Griffin is determined to make his mark, and defeat a major gang of smugglers.

## Linda Collison

## Rhode Island Rendezvous

— Adventure on the high seas in New England and the West Indies during the early days of Revolution. The third book in the popular Patricia MacPherson series.

## Water Ghosts

— *"I see things other people don't see*
*I hear things other people don't hear"* — a paranormal thriller set on board a junk peopled by troubled teens.

# Rick Spilman

## Evening Gray Morning Red
-- A young American sailor must escape his past and the clutches of the Royal Navy, in the turbulent years just before the American Revolutionary War.

## The Shantyman
— A gripping tale of survival against all odds at sea and ashore. A Kirkus Best Indie Book pick.

## Bloody Rain
— A novella of blood and madness on the Hooghly River.

## Hell Around the Horn
— The ordeal of a captain, his crew and his family in an epic doubling of Cape Horn.

# Antoine Vanner

## Britannia's Gamble

— It's 1884. A fanatical Islamist revolt is sweeping the Sudan and General Charles Gordon's hold on Khartoum is tenuous. There is only one way for Dawlish to come to the rescue — by an antique steamer, on a hostile river.

## Britannia's Amazon

— A Victorian melodrama in which Florence Dawlish, left behind in England, risks her life to save the lives of others.

## Britannia's Spartan

— A gripping yarn of convoluted diplomacy and bloody conflict in the Sea of Japan.

## Britannia's Shark

— A maritime thriller set in the time of America's Gilded Age.

## Britannia's Reach

—The action-packed second volume of the Dawlish Chronicles naval fiction series, in which Dawlish is forced to face his own conscience in a conflict of morality, in the midst of South American chaos.

## Britannia's Wolf

—An exciting debut that introduces a naval hero who is more familiar with steam, breech-loaders and torpedoes than with sails, carronades and broadsides.

# Joan Druett

Joan Druett is an independent maritime historian and writer, married to Ron Druett, a highly regarded maritime artist.

In 1984, while exploring the tropical island of Rarotonga, she slipped into the hole left by the roots of a large uprooted tree, and at the bottom discovered the grave of a young American whaling wife, who had died in January 1850 at the age of twenty-four. It was a life-changing experience. Her immediate interest in whaling captains' wives at sea was encouraged by a Fulbright fellowship, which led to five months of research in New Bedford and Edgartown, in Massachusetts, Mystic, Connecticut, and San Francisco, California, and resulted in her study of whaling captains' wives under sail, *Petticoat Whalers*.

The success of this book, and a companion volume, *She Was a Sister Sailor*, was followed by *Hen Frigates, Wives of Merchant Captains Under Sail*, which was given a New York Public Library Best to Remember Award, while *She Was a Sister Sailor* won the John Lyman Award for Best Book of American Maritime History. Joan Druett's ground-breaking work in the field of seafaring women was also recognized by a L. Byrne Waterman Award. Her non-fiction account of a double castaway experience in the sub-Antarctic, *Island of the Lost*, has become a classic in the genre. Then her strong interest in the stories of the Pacific Islanders who sailed on Euro-American ships led to a biography of an extraordinary Polynesian star navigator, *Tupaia*, which won the general nonfiction prize in the 2012 New Zealand Post Book Awards.

Joan Druett is also the author of the popular Wiki Coffin mysteries, which have a half-Maori, half-Yankee hero. Her publications, which include three romantic sagas, have been translated into Chinese, French, Italian and German.

CPSIA information can be obtained
at www.ICGtesting.com
Printed in the USA
BVHW040442090321
602012BV00007B/843

9 780992 258856